WHAT FIVE MILLION CAN'T BUY

Faith, Integrity, and the
True Definition of Winning

CORY D. SIMS

HARDCOVER ISBN: 979-8-9949583-9-1
PAPERBACK ISBN: 979-8-9949583-7-7
EBOOK ISBN: 979-8-9949583-8-4

TABLE OF CONTENTS

Preface

BEFORE THE GAME BEGINS

"Every calling begins long before the moment you answer it."

If you're holding this book, there's a good chance you've lost something before.

Maybe it was a job you prayed for and didn't get.

A relationship you believed would last forever.

A championship, opportunity, or dream you trained your whole life to win, only to come up short.

Here's what I've learned the hard way: losing doesn't mean you're finished.

In fact, sometimes losing is where the real story begins.

I learned that lesson on the biggest stage of my life: *Beast Games* Season Two.

Out of more than 400,000 applications, I was chosen as one of 200 competitors from across the United States. After weeks of pressure, sacrifice, and relentless testing, I made it all the way to the final two. The prize was five million dollars. The stakes felt like everything—my family, my future, the weight of every risk I had taken to get there.

And then . . . I lost.

That's not the ending anyone dreams about. No one grows up imagining themselves as the runner-up. There's no parade for second place. No guarantee the world will remember you kindly.

But something unexpected happened.

I didn't walk away with the money—but I walked away with something far more lasting. I walked away with the respect, encouragement, and support of millions of people who watched not just *how* I competed, but *who* I chose to be under pressure. I walked away with a deeper, stronger foundation in my faith. And I walked away with a clarity I didn't have before—about success, about purpose, and about what truly matters when everything is on the line.

This book isn't just the story of how I reached that stage.

It's the story of everything that came *before* it—the mistakes, the risks, the faith, the fear—and everything that came *after* it. It's about discovering that the scoreboard doesn't get the final say, and that sometimes life hands you a loss not to break you, but to reveal what you're made of.

I'm not here to pretend losing is easy. It isn't.

But I am here to tell you this:

There are things no amount of money can buy—integrity, peace, faith, resilience, love, and the ability to look at yourself in the mirror and know you stood firm when it mattered most.

I didn't walk away with five million dollars.

But I walked away with what five million *can't* buy.

And that's the story I want to share with you.

— Cory Sims

"I can do all things through Christ who strengthens me."
Philippians 4:13

Chapter 1
The Night Everything Changed

When a spark becomes a calling

"Sometimes destiny speaks quietly, and only those paying attention hear it."

Before I ever stepped into the competition, God planted the idea in my heart—and refused to let it go.

On the night everything changed, my life didn't look like I was a man headed toward a world-famous stage.

It looked like I was a man buried under numbers.

I was sitting at my bedroom desk late in the evening, the soft glow of a desk lamp barely cutting through the heaviness in my chest. On one side of my keyboard sat a stack of unpaid bills. On the other was a yellow notepad filled with scribbled calculations, crossed-out ideas, and half-finished plans.

Mortgage due dates.

Utility notices.

Grocery lists.

My pen hovered above the page, unmoving. I wasn't writing anymore. I was staring at the same numbers I'd stared at for months, hoping they might rearrange themselves into a miracle.

They didn't.

A year earlier, I had thrown myself into the fix-and-flip real estate world. On paper, it made sense. Buy distressed homes. Renovate them. Sell for profit. I had the work ethic. I had the drive.

What I didn't fully understand was how quickly opportunity can turn into a storm.

One project took longer than planned. Another house needed more repairs than the inspection ever hinted at. Holding costs stacked up. Interest crept higher. Materials grew more expensive. And before I realized it, the thin line between profit and disaster snapped.

There's a kind of stress that doesn't just worry you—it settles on your shoulders and steals your sleep. The kind that shows up when you're asking yourself, *How am I going to pay the mortgage?* and *What are we putting on the table for our three boys this week?*

It stopped being numbers on a page. It became my family's well-being and quality of life.

My wife, Carolina, who homeschools our boys and pours her heart into shaping their minds and their character.

Our home—our safe place.

The hardest part was knowing that many of the difficult moments we experienced traced back to my own decisions. I had stepped into business with faith and big dreams, but I had also made miscalculations. Taken risks that didn't pay off. Made choices with consequences I never expected.

From the outside, things still looked stable. I had a solid, dependable job with the federal government. It was predictable. Secure. For years, it had been our safety net.

And now it was clear: my paycheck could keep us afloat . . . barely.

But couldn't set us free.

That tension followed me everywhere.

My job whispered, *Stay safe.*

My responsibility as a husband and father demanded, *Find a way.*

And my spirit quietly urged, *Trust God—even here.*

So I did the only thing I knew how to do.

I closed my eyes, rested my hands over the messy spreadsheet of our finances, and prayed.

"Lord, I know I've made mistakes. I know I didn't always choose wisely. But You see my heart. You see my family. You see these boys who look to me for provision and protection. I don't know how You're going to do it—but I trust You. Please make a way where I can't see one."

There was no thunder from heaven. No check in the mail.

But something settled inside me—a resolute steadiness. A knowing that even when I had taken wrong turns, God hadn't abandoned me in the middle of them.

I wasn't alone at that desk.

A few minutes later, a sound pulled me from my thoughts—someone yelling from the living room. Loud. Energetic. Chaotic.

My first instinct was concern. In our home, Carolina and I are careful about what our boys watch. Whenever I hear shouting from the TV, my radar goes up.

I pushed back from my desk and walked toward the living room, the stress still clinging to me like a heavy coat—yet mixed now with curiosity.

My three boys were on the couch, eyes glued to the screen. Bright colors flashed—blues, reds, towering structures. It wasn't a cartoon. It wasn't a movie.

It was something else.

"What are you guys watching?" I asked.

"It just came on after the last show, Daddy," one of them said.

I turned toward the television—and froze.

Hundreds of people stood on towering platforms, wearing blue jerseys marked with bold white numbers. The set looked like a futuristic stage—massive scaffolding, glowing lights, enormous screens.

And at the center stood Jimmy Donaldson—MrBeast, YouTube's biggest star—commanding the moment with unmistakable purpose.

Before I realized it, I had sunk onto the couch beside my boys. Carolina joined us moments later.

For thirty-nine minutes, our living room disappeared.

Bribes. Betrayals. Sacrifices. Moments of unexpected kindness. At one point, contestants were offered a life-changing decision: take a million-dollar bribe, split among those willing to walk away.

Fifty-two people did.

Just like that, their journey ended.

I felt the question rise in my chest: *What would I do?*

Take the guaranteed money—or risk everything for something greater?

I already knew my answer. I'd stay.

I'd rather risk losing in pursuit of something meaningful than walk away early for comfort.

When the episode ended, my boys erupted with excitement. Carolina smiled. I stayed quiet.

Because while my family had watched a show, I had seen a mirror.

Pressure. Temptation. Integrity. Fear. Hope.

And beneath it all, something stirred—a spark I hadn't felt in a long time.

What if you were on that stage?

I brushed it off. I had responsibilities. Bills. A mess I was still cleaning up.

But the thought wouldn't leave.

It followed me to the gym. To my desk. Into the quiet hours of the night as I listened to my boys breathing down the hall.

If there was ever a time to lay it all on the line for them . . . it's now.

Then another conviction formed.

If I ever had the chance to compete, it wouldn't just be for us.

Over the years, I'd seen homeless veterans standing on sidewalks holding cardboard signs—men and women who once stood between us and danger. Every time, something inside me broke.

If I ever won that kind of money, it wouldn't just change my family's life. It would give others a chance to rebuild theirs.

So when applications for *Beast Games* Season Two opened, it didn't feel like opportunity.

It felt like a calling.

And I responded. I stepped away from a secure government job through a rare, delayed resignation program—burning the ships behind me with no plan B.

I was going into this competition with the mindset to win or win.

Not because it was safe.

Because it was faithful.

As I read through the application requirements, my mind exploded with ideas. I could already see the one-minute video I needed to create. It had to be something real. Something unforgettable.

I grabbed my camera and headed to the gym. Then to our chicken coop—a slice of real life, raw and unscripted. My German Shepherd sat beside me in the next shot, steady and loyal.

I ended the video talking about my favorite contestant from Season 1—Jeffrey Allen, Player 831. A man who played with integrity and fought for something far greater than money: a cure for his son Lucas, who was battling a rare genetic disorder called creatine transporter deficiency.

That kind of love stays with you.

Around that same time, I discovered another path: the Feastables sweepstakes. My boys and I turned it into a mission. Chocolate bars. QR codes. Laughter.

After a week, I realized I needed a smarter strategy unless I wanted to walk into the competition thirty pounds heavier.

I found it in the fine print. Daily registrations. Mail-in entries. Discipline.

Every application question felt like a soul check: *Why do you want to compete? What would it take for you to quit? What would you do for a million dollars?*

I answered honestly. Because this wasn't about fame.

It was about redemption, so I prayed and hit the submit button.

Then the unthinkable happened.

Exactly two hours and twenty-six minutes after I hit submit, my inbox chimed.

"Great news . . ."

My heart nearly burst.

I dropped to my knees to thank the Lord.

I scheduled the Zoom call. Completed the strength verification— pushups until my arms shook, pullups until my grip failed, leg presses until my muscles screamed.

And the next day, another email arrived:

"Congrats from Feastables!"

I froze.

Not only was I advancing through the regular application process, but I'd also won the Feastables sweepstakes.

In that moment, it all felt divine. Every late night, every prayer, and every ounce of belief had led me right here. I knew, deep down, that God had destined me to be on *Beast Games* Season 2.

I dropped to my knees and thanked God again.

Because I finally understood something I couldn't yet fully explain:

There are things five million dollars can change. And there are things it can never buy.

This journey wasn't about money. It was about obedience.

And it had only just begun.

"Oh, give thanks to the Lord, for He is good!
For His mercy endures forever."

Psalm 107:1

Chapter 2
Convincing Myself to Believe

Faith before proof

"Before anyone else believes in you, you must believe you were called."

Before the journey ever began in the sky, it began at the airport.

The car rolled to a stop at Departures, the yellow curb stretching endlessly in both directions, cars pulling in and out like lives intersecting for brief moments before moving on. I put the car in park, and for a second, no one moved. Then all three boys unbuckled at once.

They stepped out onto the concrete, the noise of rolling suitcases and overhead announcements fading as they wrapped their arms around me. One hug turned into three. Tight. Lingering. The kind you don't want to let go of because you know the moment you do, everything changes.

I felt their shoulders shake. My throat tightened. I pulled them closer, breathing them in, memorizing the weight of their heads against my chest, the sound of their voices, the feel of home in my arms.

That's when Carolina spoke—soft, steady, full of love.

"No tears, boys," she said gently. "This is a happy day for Daddy. We need to be strong."

Her words didn't erase the ache, but they gave it purpose.

Right there on the cold sidewalk—surrounded by strangers, announcements echoing overhead, wheels of suitcases humming across the floor—we bowed our heads and held hands.

Carolina prayed first. She thanked God for bringing us to this moment, for the opportunity, for His protection. She asked Him to go before me, to guard my heart, my mind, and my body, and to cover our family while we were apart.

Then each of the boys prayed—simple, honest words. For safety. For courage. For Daddy to come home. Their voices cracked, but their faith stood firm.

When it was my turn, I could barely speak. I thanked God for my family, for their strength, for trusting me enough to let me walk into the unknown. I asked Him to protect them, to guide my every step, to keep me humble, and to remind me— no matter what happened—that obedience mattered more than outcome.

When we lifted our heads, there were tears on all our faces— but also peace.

I kissed each of my sons, whispered how proud I was of them, how much I loved them. Then I turned to Carolina—my partner, my anchor, my answered prayer—and held her a moment longer than the rest.

I walked toward the airport doors without looking back, because I knew if I did, I might not keep walking.

As the plane lifted off the runway, I stared out the window and watched home fade beneath a blanket of clouds. My heart was a storm—excitement, gratitude, and the ache of leaving Carolina and the boys behind. Everything I had prayed for, trained for, and dreamed about was now in motion.

There was no turning back.

The hum of the engines became a steady reminder: I was crossing into a new chapter—one that would test more than my strength. It would test my faith. I closed my eyes, whispered a prayer, and let peace settle in.

Whatever waited on the other side, God had already gone before me.

***

Las Vegas hit like a wave the moment I stepped off the plane. The air buzzed with noise and neon. Slot machines chimed like a thousand little bells of temptation. And underneath it all pulsed something else: secrecy.

My instructions were simple—almost suspiciously simple:

Look for a sign that says "Summer Camp."

That was it. No address. No details. Just a code word in the middle of a crowded airport.

I felt like a CIA operative on a covert mission, scanning the terminal for something only a few of us would understand.

Then I saw it.

The "Summer Camp" sign stood near a smiling group from The Casting Collective, led by the ever-energetic Logan Clark. Their warmth immediately eased the tightness in my chest. They greeted me like family, not a stranger. Around us, more contestants gathered—eyes wide, walking around in that stunned state where you can't tell if you're dreaming or awake.

You could feel it: this was the beginning of something extraordinary.

Naturally, conversations started to spark. We were too excited not to talk—until a staff member gently reminded us: Not yet. At first, it felt odd, almost comical. But later, I understood. They didn't want random travelers catching wind that *Beast Games* was filming in Vegas, and they wanted those first real connections to unfold on camera—authentic, unscripted, unforgettable.

Not long after, I found myself stepping into a pink limousine with about ten other contestants, heading toward a destination only the driver knew. No one said much. But the silence spoke volumes.

When we arrived, we were escorted through a back entrance into what felt like a hidden world inside a luxury hotel. Massive ballrooms had been transformed into a full-blown command center—rows of tables, staff moving with clockwork precision, clipboards and headsets and quiet urgency everywhere.

Over the next few days, we moved through a maze of stations—medical checks, security screenings, wardrobe fittings, photoshoots, interviews. My first interview didn't go perfectly. My nerves got the best of me.

But the kindness of the staff steadied me.

Every person I met—whether from The Casting Collective or production—was professional, gracious, and genuinely supportive. The scale of it all was overwhelming, but the people made it human.

When we weren't being marched through stations, we were escorted back to our hotel rooms to rest. Phones had already been confiscated; even the phone inside the room was removed.

At first, the silence felt strange.

Then it became sacred.

With nothing to scroll, no one to call, and no way to distract myself, I did what I've always done when life gets heavy: I prayed. I read my Bible. I did pushups and sit-ups on the carpet. I mentally rehearsed challenges I hadn't even seen yet.

The game had already started—it just wasn't on camera.

Between stations, we sat in rows of chairs waiting, forbidden to talk. Staff would call out "ice" or "hard ice" whenever whispers broke out. Naturally, everybody wanted to chat—to build connections, maybe even alliances—so when attention drifted, small conversations slipped through.

"Where are you from?"

"What do you do?"

"Who are you beneath the nerves?"

Every time "ice" cut the air, I'd file those details away and jot them down later in my room. One list for names and facts. Another for potential allies. Patterns started to form—the same contestants sitting near each other, watching each other like future teammates . . . or future threats.

But my first real alliance started before all of that—back at the airport.

Standing near the "Summer Camp" sign, I scanned the crowd like a scout before battle. I watched posture. Eye contact. The way people carried themselves. Confidence reveals itself in body language long before words are spoken.

Shoulders back. Eyes forward. Calm under pressure.

That's who you want beside you when everything's on the line.

That's when I noticed him—tall, composed, unshaken. He looked staff in the eyes, every movement grounded in quiet confidence. I knew instantly: *That's someone I want on my side.*

But the rules kept us silent.

Days later, in the dining area, I saw him again—across the room, studying contestants the same way I was. Our eyes met. A wordless acknowledgment—two competitors recognizing the same fire.

As I stood to leave, he approached.

"Hey, what's up—my name's Brett."

I smiled. "Hey Brett, I'm Cory."

It was a simple exchange, but it became the start of an unbreakable alliance—one that would carry us through the toughest moments ahead . . . all the way to the top three out of two hundred.

From that point on, Brett and I moved through the process like soldiers in sync—quiet, observant, reading every detail around us. Each station felt like another test of patience and discipline, but having someone who understood the mission made all the difference. We didn't need many words. A nod or a glance said enough.

We both sensed it: something bigger was coming. A shift in the air. The calm before the storm.

Then the moment arrived.

All of us were gathered into one massive ballroom. The room quieted. The energy thickened with anticipation. Then executive producer and showrunner Sean "Klitz" Klitzner stepped forward—calm, confident, commanding the room not with force, but with presence.

That's when it hit me:

This was real.

I wasn't daydreaming anymore. I was standing on the threshold of something life-changing.

Klitz had a rare kind of leadership—genuine, humble, full of contagious energy. He didn't just speak to us; he spoke with us. He started by asking how many of us thought there were other hotels filled with contestants just like us.

Naturally, we glanced around, whispering guesses. Season 1 had begun with two thousand in Vegas. By our logic, there had to be more.

Then Klitz smiled—like he'd been waiting for us to assume wrong.

"There are only *two hundred* contestants this season."

The room gasped. The air shifted. For a moment nobody moved.

Then the realization landed: *we were the two hundred*. The chosen few. My heart raced with gratitude and awe. Out of hundreds of thousands of applications, I was standing there.

I bowed my head in thanks to my Lord Jesus.

That same night felt like something out of a movie. MrBeast rented out an entire restaurant for all of us—a private celebration to kick off the adventure. When he walked in with his team—Chandler Hallow, Nolan Hansen, Karl Jacobs, and Tareq Salameh—the room erupted in applause and laughter.

It wasn't just dinner.

It felt like the start of a family.

When I returned to my hotel room later that night, I walked into another surprise—my bed covered in gifts: a black hoodie stitched with my name and number, a *Beast Games* backpack, gear, even a Yeti and AirPods.

It felt like Christmas Eve before the biggest day of my life.

The next morning, something happened that I'll never forget.

I sat on the edge of the bed and stared at the number on my hoodie.

191.

At first, it was just a number. Then it hit me like lightning:

Psalm 91.

In that moment, I knew God was speaking to me.

He who dwells in the shelter of the Most High will rest in the shadow of the Almighty.

Peace flooded my chest. Not the kind you talk yourself into— the kind that drops into you like a gift. I felt God reminding me: *Do not fear. I will cover you. I will protect you. I will carry you.*

Out of two hundred numbers, what were the odds?

No chance—only purpose.

I jumped up, laughing and shouting with gratitude. Then I dropped to my knees and thanked the Lord for His faithfulness, for choosing me, for walking with me into this moment.

And that's when I knew the truth I'd been wrestling into belief all along:

The competition was no longer a dream.

It was destiny.

Psalm 91

He who dwells in the secret place of the Most High
Shall abide under the shadow of the Almighty.
2 I will say of the Lord, "He is my refuge and my fortress;
My God, in Him I will trust."

3 Surely He shall deliver you from the snare of the fowler
And from the perilous pestilence.
4 He shall cover you with His feathers,
And under His wings you shall take refuge;
His truth shall be your shield and buckler.
5 You shall not be afraid of the terror by night,
Nor of the arrow that flies by day,
6 Nor of the pestilence that walks in darkness,
Nor of the destruction that lays waste at noonday.

7 A thousand may fall at your side,
And ten thousand at your right hand;
But it shall not come near you.
8 Only with your eyes shall you look,
And see the reward of the wicked.

9 Because you have made the Lord, who is my refuge,
Even the Most High, your dwelling place,
10 No evil shall befall you,
Nor shall any plague come near your dwelling;
11 For He shall give His angels charge over you,
To keep you in all your ways.
12 In their hands they shall bear you up,
Lest you dash your foot against a stone.
13 You shall tread upon the lion and the cobra,
The young lion and the serpent you shall trample underfoot.

14 "Because he has set his love upon Me, therefore I will deliver him;
I will set him on high, because he has known My name.
15 He shall call upon Me, and I will answer him;
I will be with him in trouble;
I will deliver him and honor him.
16 With long life I will satisfy him,
And show him My salvation."

Chapter 3
STEPPING INTO THE ARENA

Fear doesn't disappear—it follows you forward

"Courage isn't the absence of fear, but the decision to walk anyway."

As we walked through the tunnel leading into the arena, where we would compete, the air itself seemed to vibrate. Each step echoed off the walls like a drumbeat, building anticipation with every stride. I could hear the distant hum of generators, the clatter of cameras being adjusted, and the faint murmur of crew voices on headsets calling final cues.

Then, suddenly, we stepped out of the tunnel—and the world exploded into light.

Before me stretched a stage so massive it could've been mistaken for a football field, suspended high above the ground like something out of a dream. Floodlights blazed from every direction, their beams cutting through the air like sunlight through a storm. Dozens of cameras moved in perfect synchronization—gliding across cranes and rails to capture every heartbeat, every reaction. The production crew swarmed below like an army of engineers orchestrating the impossible.

It was a sea of faces in blue uniforms, each carrying their own story . . . their own reason for being there. Some wanted money. Some wanted fame. Some wanted redemption.

I knew exactly why I was there: I wanted purpose.

I thought about the bad deals I'd made—the fix-and-flip projects that had gone sideways, the overdue notices that once sat on my desk like silent accusations. I thought about how I'd walked away from a secure government job through the delayed resignation program—burning the ships and trusting God instead of clinging to safety. I wasn't here just to win a game. I was here for Carolina. For my three boys. For the homeless veterans I couldn't forget. And for the chance to redeem the consequences of my own decisions.

But when I looked around the impressive arena, what truly stole my breath was the centerpiece—

A colossal pyramid stacked with five million dollars in real cash.

It shimmered under the lights like a mountain of promise and temptation. My pulse quickened. It wasn't just money. It was the mortgage. The loans. The weight of mistakes. The chance to rebuild and finally breathe.

And yet—even as I stared at that mountain of cash—I could feel the theme of my life tugging at me again, like God was whispering before the game even began:

Five million can change your circumstances . . . but it can't buy your soul.

Money can't buy peace. It can't buy integrity. It can't buy the kind of faith you only find when you're cornered and still choose God.

I didn't have the language for it yet, but this was already becoming the story of what five million can't buy.

As I climbed the steps onto the stage, my legs felt weightless and my heart pounded like a war drum in my chest. Every sense sharpened; I saw the brightness of the lights, felt the heat on my skin, and heard the whispers from the production crew. The platform beneath me gleamed with one hundred clear trapdoors, each one a silent question waiting to be answered:

Who will fall . . . and who will stand?

Standing there, surrounded by the magnitude of it all, I felt a surge of adrenaline unlike anything I'd ever experienced. My hands trembled—not from fear, but from awe. This was the moment I'd trained for, prayed for, and dreamed about. This was the moment that made all those late nights staring at spreadsheets, wondering how to dig myself out of the hole, feel like they had led somewhere.

And as I looked across the sea of faces, I whispered to myself, *Lord, thank You for bringing me here. Let me honor You in this competition. Let this be where You redeem what my mistakes broke.*

The challenge hadn't even begun, but I could already feel it. The test wasn't just about strength or intelligence.

It was about who you are when the lights are hottest.

Beneath those blazing beams, waiting for filming to begin, my heart pounded so hard I could almost hear it over the hum of the cameras. The air was thick with nerves, adrenaline, and electricity—the kind you can almost taste.

I looked around and couldn't help but marvel at the company I was in. Two hundred of the strongest, smartest, most determined people on the planet stood beside me. Former professional football players. Division I college stars. World's Strongest champions. Aerospace engineers from NASA and Blue Origin. Even a woman who could rattle off double- and triple-digit multiplications faster than a calculator.

Everywhere I looked, I saw excellence—people who had conquered, endured, and risen to the top of their fields.

And here we all were, united by one singular purpose: to compete for glory, to test the limits of human will, and to fight for that five-million-dollar grand prize.

But deep inside, my fight felt different.

I wasn't just trying to win money—I was trying to win *right*. I was standing there carrying the ache of real financial pressure, the weight of past missteps, and the conviction that this time I would make decisions with God, not just with ambition.

Then, through the thick air of excitement, that unmistakable voice thundered across the arena—Jimmy Donaldson. MrBeast. The man who had unknowingly sparked this entire journey months earlier.

He was exactly what you'd expect: confident, energetic, and somehow calm in the middle of the chaos. Beside him were his crew—Chandler, Nolan, Karl, and Tareq—and it was surreal seeing them in real life when my story had started watching them on a couch with my boys.

For a split second, the noise, the lights, the chaos—all of it faded.

And in that stillness, something inside me clicked.

Suddenly, I wasn't nervous anymore.

I wasn't thinking about cameras, or competition, or even the five million dollars stacked like a monument beneath him.

I was thinking about the road that brought me here—houses that flipped on me instead, nights staring at numbers that didn't add up, the humbling moment I signed my name on those resignation papers and chose to step away from safety with no plan B. I thought about the homeless veterans I'd seen on street corners and the promise I'd made, how if I ever got the chance, I would fight for them too.

And I couldn't help but laugh a little inside.

Only God could take a season of struggle and bad business decisions and turn it into an invitation from MrBeast.

As the countdown began and the first challenge was about to be revealed, I took a deep breath and smiled.

I wasn't fearless.

But I was anchored.

Because I had already made it back into the arena—not just the *Beast Games* arena, but the arena of life itself. I had chosen faith over fear, purpose over pride, and obedience over playing it safe.

And that right there was the first lesson in what five million can't buy:

A steady heart. A clean conscience. A soul that knows it's covered.

Jimmy flashed that familiar grin—the kind that somehow makes you excited and terrified at the same time.

"Welcome to the first challenge of *Beast Games* Season 2! But before we start . . . I've got some news."

Two hundred of us held our breath.

"Half of you," he said, pausing just long enough to make our stomachs drop, "will be eliminated in this very first challenge."

A collective gasp rippled across the stage. I swear I heard someone whisper, "Wait . . . half?" under their breath. My pulse spiked. You could practically feel the air tighten. All that training. All that waiting. And half of us would be gone before we even had a chance to settle in.

Classic MrBeast.

Jimmy continued, pacing with that signature mix of chaos and charm. "We've divided you into two groups: one hundred of the smartest contestants and one hundred of the strongest. Each group will face a completely different challenge. And only fifty of you from each side will survive."

The cameras zoomed in on faces—eyes wide, jaws clenched, adrenaline rising. My chest tightened, but somewhere deep inside, that old calm returned.

Psalm 91, I reminded myself. *You are covered.*

Then he explained our challenge—the one for the strong group.

Each of us would climb down a short ladder to a long, narrow pole suspended forty feet in the air. At the bottom hung a rope tied to a sandbag filled with one-third of our body weight. Our task sounded simple enough—until he finished explaining.

We had to slide down the pole, grab the rope with one hand, and—while balancing on that narrow pole—haul the sandbag up until we could reach the yellow rope. Tied to the yellow rope was a string of four small foam blocks we had to untie. Once the blocks were freed, we had to climb back up, return to the top of the stage, and stack the blocks in a precise color order before hitting the button that would lock in our spot.

Then came the part that made everyone groan.

"If you fall," Jimmy said with a grin, "you're eliminated. If your blocks fall, you're eliminated. If you stack them in the wrong color order . . . you guessed it—eliminated. And if you're not one of the first twenty-five men or twenty-five women back at the top, you're also eliminated."

The arena erupted with nervous laughter and disbelief. Someone behind me muttered, "Oh, so basically . . . don't mess up *anything.*"

I couldn't help but smile.

This was *Beast Games.*

The stakes were brutal.

And I loved every second of it.

My adrenaline surged as I stepped toward the edge of the platform and stared down at the pole below. The noise faded. My grip tightened. My heart pounded.

This was it.

The moment I had trained for, prayed for, and fought for.

Before the challenge began, I took a deep breath and stepped back from the edge. The lights and noise blurred into a distant hum. In that moment, it was just me and God.

I dropped to one knee right there on the stage and prayed—not for a spotlight win, but for a steady soul.

"Lord," I whispered, "guide my hands, steady my heart, and let Your will be done. Give me the strength to finish this race— and the peace to know You're with me every step."

When I finished, I kissed my right fist, pointed to the sky, and smiled. It wasn't for the cameras. It was my way of saying, *I'm ready, Lord. Let's do this together.*

I stood, rolled my shoulders, and tightened my grip on the small pole used to assist our descent. The stage lights glared like a thousand suns. The pole gleamed beneath me, waiting. I could feel the vibration of the cameras moving into position, the echo of producers shouting final cues, and somewhere in the background, Jimmy's voice rang out with that signature excitement that could make even fear sound fun.

"Contestants . . . are you ready?"

A wave of adrenaline surged through the air. My pulse raced, but my mind was still. I inhaled deeply and locked in.

Then came the sound that would mark the start of everything—

Jimmy yelled, "GO!"

And just like that, chaos erupted.

One hundred contestants launched into motion at once. I gripped the pole, swung my leg over, and began my descent. My hands burned against the metal as I slid down, wind whipping against my face. Grunts and shouts echoed everywhere. Bodies clattered and fell forty feet into elimination.

As I slid, my feet slammed into the round foam stopper at the bottom—harder than I expected. The impact snapped the donut clean in half, and before I could react, my body lurched downward. For a split second, I was in freefall.

Instinct took over. I landed on my sandbag and somehow managed to grab the rope, clinging with everything I had. My heart pounded so loud I could barely hear anything else.

And in that instant, I felt something so profound it stole my breath—

It felt like God's angels were holding me up, refusing to let me fall.

I froze, stunned. *What just happened?* I thought for sure I was eliminated. I had gone below the pole, and by all logic, that should've been it.

But then I looked up.

The rope was still in my hands.

The blocks were still intact.

And a thought hit me like fire:

I'm still in this.

So I steadied my grip and climbed back to the bottom of the pole. My arms trembled, but my resolve didn't.

I wasn't done.

I reached for the rope and began pulling—sandbag weight testing every ounce of strength I had. The rope groaned under tension as I hauled it higher, inch by inch. My arms burned, but I found a rhythm: pull, balance, breathe. Pull, balance, breathe.

Contestants around me were slipping, shaking, fumbling knots, panic rising.

I blocked out everything.

The blocks drew close. I untied quickly—one knot, then another, then another. Sweat dripped down my forehead, but my hands stayed steady. Before the last knot came free, I wrapped the yellow block holder around my wrist.

Then I looked up at the climb ahead.

This was the moment that separated belief from action.

I tightened my grip, whispered one more prayer, and started climbing.

Every muscle screamed as I climbed back up. The pole burned my palms. My arms shook from fatigue, but I refused to look down. The world blurred into sound—screams, metal clangs, the heavy thud of bodies falling.

None of it mattered.

One mission: get to the top.

Halfway up, I clenched my jaw and whispered, "Lord, give me strength," and pushed through the pain.

One more pull. Then another.

Then my hand hit the edge of the stage.

I hauled myself up, lungs burning, heart hammering like a drum.

I scrambled to the stacking area. My fingers felt clumsy from exhaustion, but I forced myself to slow down just enough to be precise.

First block.

Second.

Third.

Each one had to be perfect—color by color.

One mistake and everything I'd fought for would disappear.

When I placed the final block, I took one steady breath—

Then slammed my hand down on the red button.

Green lights flashed.

I had done it.

I had secured my spot for the next round.

For a moment, I just stood there—sweat pouring, hands shaking, heart overwhelmed. Celebration and heartbreak roared all around me, but all I felt was peace. Deep. Still. Humbling.

I dropped to one knee again, right there on the stage.

"Thank You, Lord," I whispered, breathless. "It was Your hand that carried me. It was You who kept me from falling."

And in that moment beneath the lights, I knew the truth:

My strength had limits.

His never did.

***

When the challenge ended, the arena erupted—celebration, heartbreak, disbelief. Some contestants shouted with joy. Others collapsed in exhaustion. Some stood frozen, stunned by the sudden finality of it all.

Half the contestants—gone.

Just like that.

The reality hit me hard. Every person out there had fought with everything they had, but the game showed no mercy.

I stood trembling from adrenaline and fatigue. Rope burns stung my hands. My pulse pounded in my fingertips. But beneath all of it was something deeper than relief:

Gratitude.

Not pride.

Not boasting.

Gratitude.

"Thank You, Lord," I whispered again. "Thank You for the strength to stand when I should have fallen."

This was more than surviving a challenge. It was God showing me in real time that the same hand that kept me from falling forty feet could also walk me out of the financial mess my own decisions helped create.

As we were escorted off the stage and back through the tunnel, the weight of the moment finally landed.

Out of two hundred, I was still standing.

But deep down, I knew this was only the beginning.

And as I walked down that tunnel, sweat-soaked and aching, one thought echoed through me like a promise:

With God beside me, there is no mountain too high and no test too great— because even five million dollars can't buy what I'm learning to carry.

The exhaustion began to fade, replaced by awe. Brett stood beside me. We'd survived. One hundred of us remained—one hundred warriors who refused to quit.

That's when Klitz stepped forward, his familiar smile cutting through the haze of lights and fatigue.

"Congratulations," he said, voice echoing. "You are officially moving on to the next stage of *Beast Games* Season 2!"

We erupted—cheers, laughter, hugs, stunned faces trying to process what had just happened. I could barely stop smiling.

Klitz continued, pride and challenge in equal measure. "You've proven your strength, your endurance, and your will to fight. But this . . ." He paused. "This was just the warm-up. The real competition begins in Beast City."

The words hit like electricity.

Beast City.

The legendary stage we had watched in Season 1—the sprawling futuristic world of lights, steel, and chaos where the impossible becomes reality.

I didn't know what waited for us there.

But I knew I wasn't walking into it alone.

"Fear not, for I am with you;
Be not dismayed, for I am your God.
I will strengthen you,
Yes, I will help you,
I will uphold you with My righteous right hand."

Isaiah 41:10

Chapter 4

WHEN FAITH MEETS THE FIRE

What Pressure Reveals

"Faith isn't tested in comfort—it's tested in the heat."

The engines roared as one hundred dreamers boarded the private charter plane that would take us to Beast City. I pressed my forehead against the window, watching the lights of Las Vegas disappear in the distance. My body ached, and my hands still burned from rope and metal, but my spirit soared.

Somewhere out there, beyond the black horizon, stood Beast City—the place where strength, strategy, and faith would be tested like never before. And as we drew closer, I could feel it in my soul: this wasn't just another challenge.

This was holy ground for anyone willing to fight for purpose.

But even as the plane cut through the sky, there was something else riding with me—something I couldn't leave behind in Vegas, something I carried from years before *Beast Games* ever entered my life.

Pain.

Not the kind you shake off after a workout. Not the kind you treat with a grin and a "walk it off."

This was *excruciating*—a deep, electric pain in my lower back that shot down my right leg like a live wire. Sciatica. Years of wear and tear from my military experience finally collecting its due, like an old injury that waits patiently until the moment you need your body most . . . and then decides to speak.

And it didn't just speak. It screamed.

Most nights, it stole my sleep. It didn't matter how exhausted I was or how badly I needed rest. I'd lie down and try to relax, and then the pain would flare, radiating through my hip, down my leg, and into my calf, like my nerves were on fire. I'd shift positions, stack pillows, stretch, breathe, pray—anything to find relief. But relief didn't always come.

There's a special kind of battle that happens at night when no one can see it—when your body won't let you rest, and your mind starts asking questions you didn't invite.

How am I supposed to compete like this?
How am I supposed to stay strong if I can't even sleep?
How am I supposed to carry a calling when my
own body feels like it's collapsing?

And right there—somewhere between the hum of airplane engines and that familiar nerve pain—I felt the message of this whole journey tightening into focus:

Five million dollars can change your life . . . but it can't buy a pain-free body.

It can't erase what you carried home from service.

It can't replace sleep.

It can't undo the cost you paid years before cameras ever rolled.

But it also can't buy what God gives a man who refuses to quit.

It wasn't lost on me that just months earlier I'd been sitting at a government desk wondering how I'd pay overdue bills from flips gone wrong. Now I was flying on a private charter into a world most people only ever see on a screen. The contrast was almost dizzying.

But that's what happens when God writes the script.

He doesn't need your circumstances to make sense before He moves.

***

The tunnel leading into Beast City glowed with a cool blue light, humming with anticipation. The sound of our footsteps echoed off the walls as we moved closer—one hundred of us, exhausted but electric with excitement. Then we crossed over into what felt like another world—a place so surreal it was as if we'd stepped off Earth and onto a different planet.

The air buzzed with electricity. The lights glowed like a living heartbeat. For a moment, it was hard to tell where reality ended and the dream began. Every step forward felt like stepping deeper into destiny itself.

Before us stretched a city that looked like something straight out of a science fiction film—futuristic, sleek, and alive. Beast City wasn't just a set; it was an entire world built from imagination and precision. Neon lights reflected off glass walls; the night sky was illuminated by LED beams that seemed to touch the stars.

Three massive pools shimmered under the lights, their turquoise water glowing against steel structures. Just beyond that was a huge outdoor workout facility—racks of weights, pull-up bars, ropes, turf fields—surrounded by a massive wall that looked impenetrable. To the right, a basketball court gleamed like polished marble beneath spotlights, and beside it, a row of cold plunges and a hot tub steamed in perfect symmetry.

The *Beast Games* logo was everywhere.

Laughter and shouts echoed as we ran out of the tunnel like kids at summer camp. Some contestants sprinted straight to the pools, jumping in fully clothed just to be the first. Others grabbed bikes and started riding around the city. Others rushed to the workout area, testing equipment, getting a feel for what looked like a utopian dream.

The energy was pure, joyful chaos—hundreds of dreams colliding in one surreal playground.

But even in the middle of that wonder, my body reminded me the battle wasn't only on the course.

As I walked, I felt that familiar sting catch in my lower back, then shoot down my right leg like someone had pulled a cord inside my spine. I kept my face steady—because that's what men do when they've learned how to function through pain. Military life teaches you to keep moving. It teaches you to grit your teeth and finish the mission.

But when the cameras aren't on and the adrenaline fades, pain becomes honest. It doesn't care who's watching.

On the other side of the city was a Feastables Café—glass-walled, glowing with bright neon colors, and stocked with every kind of snack imaginable. Right next to it was a 24/7 Starbucks, where every drink and snack was free. Contestants lined up for caramel macchiatos and double shots like they'd been stranded on an island for weeks.

I wandered deeper into the city, still in awe. There was a library lined with sleek white shelves filled with best-selling authors, and a science zone with a fully functional hydroponics garden—towers of greens sprouting under LED grow lights.

It was breathtaking—innovation mixed with imagination.

And for a man who had walked through financial stress and personal pressure, it felt like stepping into a different universe— one where God was gently reminding me, *I can still do more than you ask or imagine.*

Then we reached the sleeping pods—four massive, ultra-modern structures made of glass and steel, each housing two floors with twenty-six beds. The pods glowed softly from within, each bed neatly made with gray comforters and crisp white linens. People raced to claim bunks, laughing, shouting, calling dibs like kids on a field trip.

I just stood there, taking it all in—the laughter, the flashing lights, the sound of water splashing from the pools.

It was beautiful chaos.

For a moment, it didn't even feel like a competition. It felt like stepping into another world—one built on possibility, purpose, and childlike wonder.

I couldn't help but smile and whisper a prayer:

"Lord, thank You for bringing me here. I don't know what's ahead—but I know You're here with me."

And as I looked out over Beast City, alive with light and energy, I felt that same peace from before—the kind that only comes when you know you're standing exactly where you're meant to be.

***

As the excitement of our arrival settled, night slowly draped itself over Beast City, transforming the glowing playground into something almost peaceful. The pools shimmered beneath soft blue lights. Laughter echoed faintly in the distance. After the chaos of the day, no one was rushing, climbing, or competing; now, we were all just breathing.

Contestants sprawled across lounge chairs, dipping their feet into the pool, sipping free Starbucks drinks like it was some kind of dream resort. The tension that filled the air earlier melted into conversation, laughter, and the first threads of friendships forming.

Brett and I found ourselves surrounded by people from every walk of life—talking, laughing, and unknowingly laying the foundations for alliances that would matter later.

There was John, a firefighter from New York City, always cracking jokes in that thick accent. "Yo, what am I still doing here?" he'd say. Or, "Guys, I left my car in short-term parking at the airport. I'm gonna have to tell 'em I have to leave." We'd laugh, and somehow the pressure got lighter.

Then there was JT, another New Yorker—a police officer with a quick wit and a big heart. Between the two of them, they kept the whole group laughing even when exhaustion tried to creep in.

We met Mike, Alexis, Nate, and many others—fierce competitors but kind souls, the type who could flip from strategy to laughter in a heartbeat. Later in the game, Brett and I also joined forces with Jeff, Sue, and Emily, forming an early alliance that felt solid—though *Beast Games* would later prove alliances can shift like tides.

Toward the middle and end of the competition, as players came and went, our circle evolved. Brett and I eventually teamed up with Tyler, Nick, Auguste, and Jack—each one a powerhouse. Together, we became more than teammates. We became a brotherhood—a band of believers, dreamers, and fighters chasing something far bigger than a cash prize.

And as I watched everyone laugh under the glow of Beast City's lights, I couldn't shake the feeling none of it was random. These weren't just contestants.

They were people God had intentionally placed in my path.

In a city built for competition, God was quietly building connection—and that reminder filled me with peace.

*****

Inside the sleeping pods, the energy was still electric. Some contestants claimed beds like they were in a dorm room. Others lay back staring at the ceiling lights, still trying to believe this was real.

I sat on my bed for a moment, looking around at the faces of people who had been strangers just days earlier; now, they were teammates, rivals, and friends. I thought about the scriptures Carolina had shared with me before I left—about God's promise to uphold me with His righteous right hand.

I could feel that promise even here.

But then night came—and the real test arrived.

Because Beast City may have looked like paradise, but my body didn't care how pretty the lights were.

When the pod quieted and the chatter faded, I laid down and tried to let my muscles finally relax. I wanted rest. I needed it. But within minutes, the sciatica pain flared again. My lower back tightened, and the nerve fire ran down my right leg. I shifted. Rolled to one side. Then the other. Tried to breathe through it.

The kind of pain that keeps you awake doesn't just steal sleep—it steals patience. It steals comfort. It steals your sense of control.

And in that darkness, while the city outside glowed like a dream, I felt myself face another truth:

Five million dollars couldn't buy what I needed most in that moment: relief.

It couldn't purchase a full night of sleep. It couldn't undo what years of service had etched into my spine.

But God could give me something else: strength. Endurance. Peace that doesn't depend on comfort.

So I opened my Bible and prayed. Psalm 91 had become my anchor—my nightly declaration. I read it every night before closing my eyes and every morning when I woke, reminding my soul that I was covered, protected, and never walking this path alone.

Tomorrow, the next challenge would come—new tests, new battles, new lessons in faith.

But that night in Beast City, with pain running through my leg and the lights humming outside the pod, I realized something deeper:

This wasn't just a competition against other contestants.

This was a proving ground.

Not to see *if* I had what it took—God already knew I did—but to show me what I'd been carrying all along. That the same discipline the military forged in me, the same resolve fatherhood demanded from me, and the same faith that kept me steady at my desk back home . . . All of it was still there, even when my body screamed and sleep wouldn't come.

I've never quit at anything in my entire life, and I wasn't about to begin quitting now.

The only question was what kind of man I would be in the suffering—what kind of spirit I would carry when comfort was gone and the cameras weren't there to make it cinematic.

So I laid there in the dark, breathing through the pain, and I did what I've always done: I anchored myself to God.

Because I hadn't come this far to wonder if I could endure.

I'd come to endure—and to do it with integrity, humility, and faith.

***

The next few days in Beast City felt like a surreal slice of paradise tucked inside the competition of a lifetime. With no phones, no outside distractions, and nothing to focus on except faith, friendship, and the game ahead, life took on a rhythm that felt almost timeless.

Mornings began with laughter across the courtyard, sneakers squeaking on the basketball courts, and the smell of fresh coffee drifting from the 24/7 Starbucks. Contestants worked out together in the open-air gym, spotting each other on lifts, cheering on personal bests, and turning training into therapy. We pushed each other—harder, faster, stronger—not just as rivals, but as people chasing something greater than ourselves.

In the evenings, people sat around the pool or the library, trading stories about families, faith, and dreams. Some played chess, cards—anything to pass the time and keep their mind sharp. That's where I met Omar, one of the smartest and kindest people in Beast City. He taught me chess with patience, explaining every move like it was a life lesson. I told him my boys were amazing chess players and that I couldn't wait to go home and challenge them with what I'd learned. He laughed and said, "Then we'd better make sure Dad can hold his own."

It was moments like that—the small, human ones—that made Beast City feel less like a competition and more like a community.

But deep down, we all knew the calm couldn't last.

Because in *Beast Games*, pressure always returns.

And when it does, it doesn't just test what you can do.

It reveals who you really are—especially when you're hurting, exhausted, and still choosing faith anyway.

> *"He only is my rock and my salvation;*
> *He is my defense;*
> *I shall not be greatly moved."*
>
> **Psalm 62:2**

Chapter 5
Training for More Than a Game

**Preparing the body,
sharpening the spirit**

"What you do in private determines who you become in public."

The calm in Beast City couldn't last forever. Deep down, we all knew it. After days filled with laughter, training, and a dreamlike peace, something shifted in the air—subtle at first, like the pressure change before a storm. The lights felt a little brighter. The energy grew a little heavier. Everyone could feel it: the game was about to demand more.

And then the call came.

All one hundred of us were summoned again. Together, we walked through the glowing portal toward the next challenge. None of us knew what waited on the other side, but we all knew this was a turning point. Whatever happened next would separate intention from resolve.

We stepped onto a stage that felt part game show, part science fiction. Steel, light, bright white. Jimmy walked out with that familiar grin—the one we already knew meant chaos was coming.

"All right, contestants," he said, pacing slowly. "For this next challenge, I've got an offer. A little temptation."

He paused.

"If you choose to walk away right now, you'll leave *Beast Games* . . . but you'll walk away with one hundred thousand dollars."

The stage erupted.

A hundred thousand dollars. For many, that money would be life-changing. It would be for me, too. I knew exactly what that money could do—erase some of the scars left by failed flips, quiet the overdue notices, relieve pressure I'd carried for far too long.

There was a time when that number would've felt like salvation.

But this time, the words hit differently. I felt it in my chest before I felt it in my head.

Instinctively, I knew I was here for something else. Something money can't buy.

Around me, voices rose as contestants calculated in real time. You could see the struggle written on faces—the pull between relief and risk, safety and calling. I understood the tension. I'd lived it. I'd chased short-term fixes before, convinced they'd solve long-term problems.

They never did.

My decision didn't take thought.

I wasn't here for a bribe. I wasn't here for relief disguised as surrender. I'd trained too long, prayed too hard, and carried too much pain—physical and spiritual—to walk away now. My integrity wasn't for sale. Not for a hundred thousand dollars. Not for any number.

Jimmy smiled wider. "But wait," he said. "There's a twist."

Ten guards stood behind him, masked and silent, each holding a silver briefcase. The lights caught the metal just right—clean, sharp, tempting. Then Jimmy raised his voice.

"Guards . . . reveal yourselves!"

The masks came off—and the place exploded.

As the noise surged, it finally registered who they were.

Returning players—but not just any players. They were legends.

At the center stood Jeff, the winner of *Beast Games* Season 1—and my favorite contestant from that season. He wasn't just competing for himself; he was fighting for a cause far greater than the game. Jeff played every challenge with heart, grit, and quiet determination because waiting for him back home were his wife Jennifer, his son Jack, and his other son, Lucas, who lives with a rare neurological condition called creatine transporter deficiency (CTD). CTD is a genetic disorder that affects the brain's ability to transport creatine, a compound essential for energy and normal brain function. Children with

CTD often face developmental delays, speech impairments, seizures, and lifelong neurological challenges. Watching Jeff carry that weight and still compete with integrity and love showed me what it truly means to fight with purpose. He didn't just outlast everyone; he proved that when the cause is bigger than the prize, endurance takes on a whole new meaning.

Standing beside him was Twana, the Season 1 runner-up—strong, composed, and relentless, someone who had come within inches of winning it all.

Then there was Gage, forever etched into *Beast Games* history as the man who flipped the coin that doubled the grand prize from five million dollars to ten million. One decision. One moment. A reminder of how quickly everything could change.

Mia stood proudly among them, the contestant who won an island worth $1.8 million—a victory that felt straight out of a dream. Courtney and JC, both top-ten finishers from Season 1, carried themselves with the natural confidence of people who had survived deep into the game and understood exactly what it demanded.

I spotted Deano and Jeremy, two men whose integrity had defined their journeys. They had both turned down one million dollars—deliberately—choosing loyalty to their team over personal gain. That kind of decision leaves a mark on a man.

Akira stood nearby as well, unmistakable; he was the winner of a Lamborghini in Season 1 and a key contributor in some of the most pivotal challenges of the entire competition. His presence reminded everyone that *Beast Games* rewarded more than brute strength; it rewarded impact.

And then there was Karim.

Karim had taken a lot of heat during Season 1. Public opinion hadn't been kind. But here he was—back not for money or attention, but for redemption. For the chance to rewrite a story that hadn't ended the way he wanted. Seeing him there was proof that *Beast Games* wasn't just about winning; it was about second chances.

Standing there, watching them step forward, I felt something deeper than excitement. These weren't just contestants filling spots. They were living proof of what this arena could forge—men and women shaped by pressure, tested by temptation, and refined by the choices they made when everything was on the line.

This wasn't a twist for entertainment.

It was a reminder.

The game remembers who you are when the money is loud—and when integrity is quiet.

"If you take the $100K," Jimmy continued, "you're eliminated—but you get to choose one of these ten to take your place."

Chaos. Cheers. Disbelief.

Ten contestants from our season took the deal. Ten chose certainty over calling. And just like that, the Season 1 players stepped back into the game.

I stood there quietly, absorbing it all.

Only in *Beast Games.*

But beneath the noise, I felt that familiar calm—the peace that comes when you know you're walking the right road. My journey wasn't about shortcuts anymore. I'd learned where that road led. This season of my life wasn't about fixing mistakes quickly; it was about becoming someone steady enough not to repeat them.

Obedience over impulse. Purpose over pressure.

That mattered more than money.

Once the excitement settled, Jimmy spoke again.

"Contestants, you will now choose which challenge you'll compete in. Your options are: Balls, Balance, Blocks, or Bluff."

Four words. No explanations.

The names glowed on the floor, paired with cryptic symbols that revealed nothing. People whispered, guessed, tried to out-think the moment. I didn't.

I lowered myself to one knee to pray.

"Lord," I prayed quietly, "guide me. Let Your will—not mine—decide."

In the stillness, the answer came without noise.

Blocks.

No logic. No calculation. Just obedience.

I stood, stepped forward, and made my choice.

And in that moment—long before I knew what the challenge would require—I understood something clearly:

Sometimes the decision that changes everything isn't loud or dramatic. Sometimes it's a quiet act of trust. A willingness to follow God even when your body hurts, your future feels uncertain, and the easier option is standing right in front of you.

That choice—made on a stage under bright lights, with pain in my leg and peace in my chest—would carry me further than I ever imagined.

Because I wasn't training for a game anymore.

I was training for what five million could never buy.

"This is love, that we walk according to His commandments. This is the commandment, that as you have heard from the beginning, you should walk in it."

2 John 1:6

Chapter 6
Leaving Home to Chase the Call

The cost of obedience

"Every great pursuit requires leaving something behind."

We walked back through the glowing portal and re-entered Beast City, the air thick with anticipation. Crew members guided us toward a massive open sand pit surrounded by cranes, floodlights, and giant foam-colored blocks. The scale alone told us this wouldn't be simple—and nothing in *Beast Games* ever was.

As I crossed the sand, curiosity tugged at me. Two enormous cranes loomed overhead, each with a flag dangling fifty feet in the air. The blocks were oversized, awkward, and heavy—part construction site, part puzzle, part chaos waiting to be unleashed. Whatever this challenge was, it would demand more than strength. It would demand leadership.

Then Jimmy walked out, smiling like a man who knew exactly how much pressure he was about to drop into the pit.

"For this challenge," he said, "we're going to pick two captains—one from the smart team, and one from the strong."

As he explained how the captains would be chosen, a realization hit me. My time in the first strong challenge had been fast—maybe the fastest.

By God's grace, I was chosen as one of the captains.

The moment landed heavy—not with pride, but with responsibility. I had led before in my life—in the military, on job sites, in business deals, in decisions I thought would secure our future. Some of those choices had cost us dearly. Standing there now, chosen to lead in front of the world, I felt the Lord whisper clearly: *This time, don't lean on your own understanding. Lead with Me.*

This wasn't about winning money. It was about stewarding influence—something five million dollars could never buy.

Then came the real test: building the team.

The contestants stood divided—the strong, the smart, and the OGs from Season 1. No rules yet, but I knew this would be a team challenge. I prayed on one knee, as always, asking God to order my steps.

Jimmy flipped a coin. Yellow—my team.

"Favor," I whispered.

I chose the same way I'd chosen everything so far: through obedience. Strength first. Foundation before finesse.

My first pick was Mitch—pure power with a disciplined mind. Then Colby, steady under pressure. Nicky—fast, focused, fearless. Ella—athletic and composed. From there, I balanced experience with intellect: JC for leadership, Sophia fresh out of law school, Trina the engineer with the same IQ as Einstein, Sue with Survivor instincts forged under pressure. One by one, the team came together—Jordan, Hannah, Mike, Brandon, Omar, Michelle, Inaam, Kady, Ethan, Michelle, Joseph, and Luke—not just capable, but cohesive.

When the teams were set, Jimmy announced the challenge.

"Stack your blocks high enough to grab the flag. Limited blocks. Choose wisely."

Fifty feet in the air. No margin for error.

I pulled my team into a circle. "We build fast—but we build right. Stability first. No shortcuts."

As I spoke, memories surfaced—houses I'd rushed, deals built on optimism instead of wisdom. I wasn't repeating that mistake here.

Before the horn sounded, I dropped to one knee in the sand and prayed—for wisdom, clarity, and humility.

Then chaos erupted.

Blocks were dragged, ropes hauled, voices shouted. Mitch and Evelyn sprinted like warriors. Colby took the rope, hauling blocks skyward. Trina called commands with surgical precision. Every movement mattered.

Hours passed. Night faded into dawn. Hands blistered. Muscles screamed. No one quit. No one complained.

When Colby finally faded, Mitch climbed. Fifty feet up, pulling block after block, steady and relentless.

Johnny's team was close. Their structure wobbled but held.

Then Jimmy's voice thundered: "The flags will begin lowering— one foot every ten minutes."

Mitch waited. Johnny jumped too soon.

The miss sucked the air from the pit.

Seconds later, our flag dropped just enough.

Mitch grabbed it.

We won.

Cheers exploded. Sand flew. I dropped to one knee again—not because of victory, but because I knew the truth.

This wasn't just about stacking blocks.

It was about rebuilding a life the right way—on faith, patience, and obedience. About learning that what five million can't buy is the wisdom to build something that lasts.

As the sun rose over Beast City, painting the sky gold, we walked back exhausted, blistered, and victorious. But deeper than the adrenaline was peace—the kind that comes from knowing you chose the hard road and honored God in the process.

Because when God is your cornerstone, even the tallest towers stand firm.

Christ Our Cornerstone

19 Now, therefore, you are no longer strangers and foreigners, but fellow citizens with the saints and members of the household of God, 20 having been built on the foundation of the apostles and prophets, Jesus Christ Himself being the chief cornerstone, 21 in whom the whole building, being fitted together, grows into a holy temple in the Lord, 22 in whom you also are being built together for a dwelling place of God in the Spirit.

Ephesians 2:19–22

Chapter 7

Beast City

**Entering a world
built to break you**

"Not every battlefield looks like a war zone."

Fifty contestants. That's all that remained.

The once-crowded areas of Beast City felt different now—quieter, sharper, more focused. The laughter was still there, but it carried a new weight. Every conversation, every handshake, every smile came with an unspoken understanding: We were deep in the game now. The finish line wasn't just a dream anymore; it was somewhere out there on the horizon, waiting for those strong enough to reach it.

Our camaraderie had grown tighter with each challenge. The bonds forged in the fire of competition had become something real—deeper than strategy, stronger than convenience. And now, with some of the OGs from Season 1 among us—Jeff, JC, and Mia—the atmosphere shifted in the best way possible. Their presence brought wisdom, steadiness, and heart. It felt like the next generation had merged with the last, creating a new kind of unity.

Brett and I, especially, found ourselves growing close to Jeff. From the moment we met him, it was clear there was something special about him. Jeff didn't just carry experience; he carried perspective. There was a calm about him, the kind that only comes from walking through fire and coming out refined. He felt like an older brother—one who had already seen the battlefield and was sent, by God's own design, to guide us through ours.

One afternoon, Jeff pulled me aside, away from the noise and chatter. He looked me square in the eyes with that mix of kindness and conviction that only he could carry and said, "Cory, you're a great guy, and everyone loves you because of your kind heart. But there's going to come a point where you'll have to play hard."

At first, I didn't fully understand what he meant. I nodded, tucked those words somewhere deep in my mind, and carried on. But something in the way he said it—the gravity in his tone—made me feel like it wasn't advice from man, but a message from God Himself.

I thought back to my life before *Beast Games*—times I'd played too safe at my government job, clinging to security, and other times I'd swung too recklessly in business deals without truly seeking God's wisdom. Jeff wasn't telling me to abandon integrity. He was calling me to Spirit-led courage. Not fear masked as wisdom. Not recklessness masked as faith. But obedience with a backbone.

It wouldn't be until much later, during the phone bribe challenge, that those words would come roaring back to the surface. When I faced a moral crossroads—choosing between playing it safe or risking it all—Jeff's voice echoed in my heart. *Play hard.* That was the moment I realized exactly what he meant.

But that revelation would come later. For now, we had another mission ahead.

***

Jimmy gathered us together, his voice booming over the speakers. "Contestants," he announced, "you're about to face your next challenge. You'll need to form teams of five—but there's a twist. Each team must include at least *two smart players.*"

Instantly, the peaceful rhythm of Beast City turned into organized chaos. Contestants scrambled, whispering and strategizing, trying to find their perfect mix of muscle and intellect. Brett and I looked around at the familiar faces of our crew; John and JT had been with us from the beginning, but the new rule meant we'd have to split. It stung, but we knew it was part of the game.

As Brett and I searched for who to team up with next, something incredible happened. It was as if the Red Sea parted right before us—and standing there on the other side were Jeff, Sue, and Emily, huddled together and looking for two more to complete their team.

The second our eyes met, we all smiled. No words needed.

It was one of those divine moments where you just *know*. The kind that doesn't need explanation because it's too perfect to be coincidence. God had His hand in it—guiding, aligning, orchestrating.

And just like that, our team of five was formed. Faith, strength, wisdom, experience, and heart—all standing together, ready for whatever was coming next.

The teams were instructed to each stand on one of ten numbered platforms—five contestants per team. The numbers glowed beneath our feet in brilliant color, like ten launchpads ready to send us into whatever madness lay ahead.

Jeff didn't hesitate for a second. He led our team straight to Platform Six. It was poetic—and, honestly, divine. He had won *Beast Games* Season 1 holding briefcase number six. Seeing him step onto that same number again felt like a full-circle moment, one only God could write. I could feel His hand in it—a reminder that He doesn't deal in coincidences; He deals in purpose.

Once all ten teams were in position, Jimmy walked to the center of the stage, standing beside a massive spinning wheel marked with numbers one through ten. That familiar spark in his eyes told us everything—something wild was coming.

"All right, contestants," he began, his voice booming across the city. "Here's how this next challenge is going to work. Chandler is going to spin this wheel, and whichever number it lands on will get to choose which other team they'll compete against."

Heads turned. Eyes darted. You could practically feel everyone thinking the same thing: *Compete how?*

Jimmy grinned, almost reading our minds. "Oh, and by the way," he added, "you still don't know what the actual challenge is."

Laughter rippled nervously through the contestants, but beneath it was tension, sharp and electric. Fifty of the strongest, smartest, and most determined people in the world stood on glowing platforms, waiting to face a mystery we couldn't prepare for.

Chandler gave the wheel a powerful spin. The lights flashed. The numbers blurred. Every eye followed as it clicked past each slot—5 . . . 7 . . . 9 . . . slowing . . . slowing . . . until it finally stopped on number one.

A collective gasp filled the air. Team One looked at each other, exchanged a few quick whispers, then confidently chose to face Team Five.

Jimmy reset the wheel. Another spin. It clicked past 2 . . . 4 . . . 6 . . . slowing again . . . until it stopped on number eight.

Team Eight looked at each other, exchanged a few quick whispers, then confidently chose to face Team Three.

Jimmy reset the wheel. Another spin. It clicked past 6 . . . 7 . . . 9 . . . slowing again . . . until it stopped on number two.

Team Two. The group led by Mitch, with Colby, Sophia, Jessie, and Morgan by his side. My heart gave a strange twist.

Those were my former teammates—the same warriors I had fought beside in the *Blocks* challenge. My brothers and sisters in battle.

Jimmy turned to them with that trademark grin. "Team Two," he said, "who are you going to face?"

Everything fell silent. Mitch, Colby, Sophia, and Morgan exchanged glances—a silent conversation only teammates could have. Then, slowly, their eyes drifted toward us.

I could feel their gaze before I even saw it. I smiled faintly, already sensing what was about to happen.

Jimmy leaned forward. "So . . . what's your choice?"

With a mix of hesitation and mischief, they said it. "Team Six."

Our team.

The reaction was instant—gasps, laughter, shouts echoing across the city. For a split second, I found it peculiar. Why us? We'd fought together just days ago. But this was *Beast Games*; alliances here were like shifting sand. The line between friend and foe could change with a single spin of a wheel.

I took a slow breath and steadied my heart. I wasn't going to let pride or bitterness take root. I knew where that path led— and it wasn't victory.

Instead, I whispered under my breath, *"Lord, keep my heart pure and my focus clear. Help me fight with strength, not spite."*

The wheel continued to spin until all the matchups were set, each new pairing sparking another round of cheers and nerves.

Then Jimmy stepped forward again, that familiar grin spreading across his face as the city went silent. My pulse quickened, and that same rush of anticipation flooded my chest. Everyone waited for him to explain what would come next. But instead of giving us the rules, Jimmy simply said, "Teams One and Five—step forward."

Without another word, both teams marched out of Beast City and into the unknown. No explanation. No clue what they were walking into. Just faith and adrenaline guiding their steps.

The rest of us stood in the sand pit area, staring at each other in confusion. Whispers broke out. "What kind of challenge is it?" "Is it physical? Mental? A puzzle?" Nobody knew. We watched as the two teams disappeared into the darkness.

A few minutes later, the massive screen in the center of Beast City flickered on—and that's when we finally saw it.

The image that appeared looked like something out of a dream . . . or a nightmare, depending on how you saw it. A sprawling obstacle course stretched across what looked like a huge lake. It was pure madness—like *American Ninja Warrior* and *Wipeout* had collided into one impossible creation. Giant windmills spun like helicopter blades, narrow beams crossed over the water, and slick platforms waited like traps, daring someone to be overconfident.

It was beautiful and brutal all at once.

But here's the thing: We could *see* everything, but we couldn't *hear* anything. The audio was off. No commentary, no rules, no Jimmy. Just the visuals. We were left to piece together what was happening through movement and chaos.

We leaned forward, eyes locked on the screen. Two figures appeared at the starting line—one from each team. Even without sound, I could tell who they were: JT and Avery.

The horn must've sounded, because both men suddenly launched forward. They leaped across the first set of narrow beams and then jumped to the platforms. The windmills were monstrous—massive paddles sweeping through the air like wrecking balls.

Then, in one split second, it happened. Avery misjudged the final jump, and he dropped straight into the water below. Even without sound, the splash looked catastrophic. Just like that, his entire team was eliminated.

JT reached the final platform, hit the button, and raised his arms in victory. Even though we couldn't hear it, we could *feel* the roar of celebration.

One matchup down—and already the atmosphere was shifting. The energy felt unstable, electric, like chaos was just beginning to stretch its legs.

It was in that brief pause between rounds that I had a conversation I'll never forget.

Nicole—contestant 186—pulled me aside. Her voice was calm, steady, but her eyes carried a certainty that stopped me in my tracks. She told me she felt the Lord place a verse on her heart.

Proverbs 3:26.

"For the Lord will be your confidence,
And will keep your foot from being caught."

She looked at me and said she believed it wasn't just for her—that the Holy Spirit was speaking directly to me about the obstacle course ahead. About footing. About trust. About moving forward without fear.

The words settled deep inside me, anchoring my spirit in the middle of the noise. I held on to them like a promise.

And then Jimmy's voice rang out again.

"Next up—Team Eight versus Team Three."

The game moved on. But the message stayed with me.

We all straightened up when we saw Monika on the screen; she was one of the strongest athletes among us. A former gymnast, she moved with pure poetry. From the second she started, it was like watching grace in motion. Where others hesitated, she flowed. Where others stumbled, she soared.

Every competitor in the city stood frozen, mouths slightly open, watching her glide through the course. She didn't just finish it; she *commanded* it. It was art in motion, and I found myself smiling, shaking my head. *That's exactly how it's done.*

And then . . . our turn was up.

Team Two vs. Team Six.

My heart skipped a beat. The crowd around us murmured as Brett gave me a firm pat on the shoulder, Jeff nodded calmly, and I closed my eyes for just a second.

Lord, I prayed silently, *You've brought me this far. Give me focus, give me strength, and let Your will be done.*

This was it—the moment we would face the very teammates I had once fought beside.

As we marched out the city walls into the unknown, I could feel it—that quiet, burning certainty that faith, not fear, would carry me through whatever storm waited on the other side of that starting line.

The vans rumbled down the dusty road, headlights slicing through the nightly haze as we left the glowing walls of Beast City behind. None of us spoke much during the ride—there was a subdued electricity in the air, that mix of nerves and anticipation that always comes before something big. We didn't know exactly where we were headed, but we could feel the weight of it. Every second brought us closer to another test— another moment where faith and fear would collide.

When the vans finally stopped, the doors opened to reveal the obstacle course in full view. It stretched across a field like something built for titans—massive beams, spinning windmills, and a lake of water shimmering under the floodlights below. It looked even more intense up-close than it had on the screen back in the city.

Before we climbed the steps to the starting platform, Jeff called us together. He placed his hand on my shoulder and said quietly, "Let's pray."

So right there, at the foot of that towering structure, we all bowed our heads. Jeff led us in prayer—asking for strength, focus, and protection. He prayed that whatever happened next would bring glory to God, not to us. It was calm, but powerful—like the eye of a storm before the wind returns.

As we climbed the stairs, the lights grew brighter and the energy pressed in around us. Jimmy stood waiting at the top, smiling in that way that meant something wild was about to happen.

"All right," he said, pacing in front of us. "Do you understand the rules?"

We glanced at each other.

"Not exactly," I admitted with a nervous grin.

He laughed. "Good. Every challenge has its own twist—and this one's no different."

Then he turned serious. "For this challenge, it's captain versus captain. One competitor from each team will run the course. Whoever crosses the finish line first secures their entire team's spot in the game. The other team . . . goes home."

The weight of his words settled heavily on my chest. I looked at my teammates—Brett, Jeff, Sue, and Emily—and then at the monstrous course ahead.

That's when Brett and Jeff turned to me. Steady and sure, they said, "You're the one, Cory. You've got this. I believe in you."

Sue and Emily nodded. "We all do."

I looked up at the night sky. The wind moved gently across my face, and in that still moment, I felt it—that divine pull in my spirit. God wasn't whispering anymore. He was calling.

I nodded. "All right," I said quietly. "Let's do this."

There was no backup plan here—no safety net, no "I'll just fall back on my old job" option. I had left that life behind when I signed the delayed resignation papers. Just like in my real life, this course was win-or-win—not in the sense that I had to come in first place, but in the sense that I had to honor God and give everything I had, no holding back.

Then something profound happened on that platform.

As we stood there preparing for the challenge, Emily spoke softly. "I'm not really a believer," she said, "but . . . I can feel something here. Something powerful."

Her words sent a chill through me. I knew exactly what she felt—it was the presence of the Holy Spirit, filling that space, wrapping around us like armor. God was there.

I dropped to one knee and bowed my head. "Lord," I prayed, "be with me. Guide my steps. Let Your will be done, not mine."

When I rose, Jimmy's voice broke through the silence again.

"Oh, and one more thing," he said with that signature grin. "There's a twist. If anyone wants to switch sides—if you think the other captain is going to win—now's your chance."

Without hesitation, my team all dropped to one knee behind me. Every single one of them. A silent, unshakable show of faith.

That moment hit me hard—right in the heart. I'll never forget it. It wasn't just loyalty; it was love, faith, and trust all wrapped into one beautiful gesture.

Then Jimmy yelled, "Go!"

I launched forward onto the first beam—long, narrow, and shaking under my weight. My arms instinctively reached for balance as the wind hit my face. Every movement demanded focus. Every second mattered.

I started moving faster, bounding from platform to platform, the lights flashing and water churning below. I could hear Jimmy's voice echoing faintly through the speakers—"Colby's in the lead!"

That lit something inside me—a fire straight from heaven. I could feel my spirit roar awake. I wasn't just running for me anymore; I was running for them—for my team, my family, my faith.

I pushed harder, my legs pumping, arms swinging, breath sharp and steady. It felt like God's angels were carrying me, lifting me through every obstacle, giving me strength beyond my own.

As I reached the final stretch, I saw Colby out of the corner of my eye—strong, fast, relentless. But in that instant, everything slowed. My heart, my thoughts, the noise around me—gone. There was only light, movement, and faith.

And then . . . I leaped.

My foot hit the final platform just before Colby's did. The button flashed, the lights erupted, and the roar of victory filled the air.

I immediately pointed to the sky, shouting and laughing all at once. "Thank You, Lord!" I yelled, "All glory to You!"

I knew with every fiber of my being that I hadn't done that alone. God had been with me every single step of the way.

When I looked over at Colby, he smiled—pure respect in his eyes. He was an incredible athlete, a fierce competitor, and a good man. I went and gave him a big hug and said quietly, "Amazing run, brother, so much respect for you."

Because in that moment, even standing in victory, I knew—the real triumph wasn't just crossing the finish line. It was feeling God's presence in the middle of the storm and realizing that faith, not fear, had carried me across.

The horn had barely finished echoing when the cheers erupted. My team came sprinting down the sidelines toward the finish line—Jeff, Brett, Sue, and Emily, their faces lit up with joy and disbelief. We collided in a wave of shouts, laughter, and hugs. The adrenaline was still pounding through my veins, my chest heaving, my legs trembling, but all I could do was lift my hands to the sky.

"All glory to God!" I shouted over the noise. "He did it! Not me—Him!"

Jeff clapped me on the back, his grin wide. "Brother, that was *unbelievable!* You just took down one of the best!"

Brett pulled me into a bear hug. "I told you, man. I knew you were the one. You had that fire in your eyes."

Sue laughed, shaking her head. "That was insane! You were flying out there!"

Even Emily—the one who had said earlier she wasn't a believer—looked at me and said softly, "I don't know what that was, but . . . I *felt* it."

Her words nearly brought me to tears. Because I knew exactly what it was. It wasn't luck. It wasn't coincidence. It was the Holy Spirit—alive, present, and powerful.

As we made our way down from the platform, the other teams who had already won their heats stood along the sidelines, clapping and cheering. JT came up, gave me a big hug, and said, "That was one of the craziest comebacks I've ever seen."

Monika grinned. "You looked like you had wings out there!"

I laughed, still breathless. "I did," I said, pointing upward. "They were just invisible."

Standing there among champions, the cool air brushing against my skin, I felt the weight of it all—the exhaustion, the joy, the gratitude. My heart was still racing, but it wasn't from nerves anymore. It was from *awe*.

I hadn't felt a victory like that in years—not since before the setbacks, not since before life had tested me in ways I never saw coming. This wasn't just a win on a scoreboard. It was a reminder of what faith and perseverance can do when they walk hand in hand.

I looked out across the course—the same one that had nearly sent me falling into the water minutes before—and whispered quietly, "Thank You, Lord. Thank You for catching me when I can't catch myself."

And as the next teams stepped up to face their own battles, I stood there beside my team—alive, humbled, victorious— knowing deep down that this was far more than a competition.

It was a testament.

A testament to what happens when you trust that God's angels can carry you further than your own strength ever could.

***

By the time we returned to Beast City, the night sky had settled deep and still, but my heart hadn't. The adrenaline was still pulsing through my veins like electricity. Every time I replayed that finish in my mind—that final leap, that moment of grace—I felt a wave of awe rush over me all over again. I tried to lie down, but sleep wouldn't come. My body was still buzzing, my spirit wide awake. So I just sat there in the quiet of my bunk, hands clasped, whispering prayers of thanksgiving. "Thank You, Lord," I said over and over, "for giving me strength when I had none, for guiding every step, for showing me once again that with You, all things are possible."

"But Jesus looked at them and said to them,
"With men this is impossible,
but with God all things are possible."

Matthew 19:26

Chapter 8
ALLIANCES AND TRUST

Strength multiplied

"No one reaches the summit alone."

I woke up the next morning still riding the high of victory. My body was tired, but my heart felt alive—overflowing with gratitude, joy, and awe.

Before my feet even touched the floor, I bowed my head and prayed. "Thank You, Lord, for another day in this city, for another chance to glorify You. Whatever comes next, let Your will be done, not mine."

I read Psalm 91, as I always did.

The air inside Beast City felt different that morning. The once-bustling city was now calm and almost sacred. Only twenty-five contestants remained. The pools sat still, the Feastables Café hummed quietly, and the laughter that used to echo across the city was now replaced by soft footsteps and whispers.

You could feel it—the calm after a battle.

And deep down, I knew what that calm always meant in *Beast Games*. Another storm was coming.

Sure enough, just as the sun went down that evening, Jimmy's voice broke through the speakers across the city.

"Contestants," he said, "meet me at the sand pit."

I took a deep breath, feeling that familiar blend of anticipation and peace. *Lord, guide me,* I prayed silently as we walked through the city toward the open sand pit.

When we arrived, the sand pit looked completely transformed. The towering obstacles from past challenges were gone. In their place stood five circular podiums, evenly spaced like stones in an ancient arena. The setup felt simple—but the simplicity made it even more unnerving.

Jimmy stood waiting, hands clasped, a smile tugging at the corner of his mouth—the kind that always meant something unpredictable was about to happen.

"Step up onto a podium with your team," he said. "This next one's called The Captain's Bribe."

Just hearing the word *bribe* sent a ripple through the group.

For me, it cut deeper.

Knowing what it felt like to chase "quick fixes"—to think one deal, one flip, one risky move could erase a trail of bad decisions—had changed me. In the past, I had lived that mindset. I had watched it cost me more than it ever gave me. That's why, standing there in Beast City, staring at five podiums and hearing the word *bribe*, I could feel the heartbeat of this book forming in real time:

What five million can't buy is a clean conscience.

It can't buy peace at night.

It can't buy the kind of integrity that holds when pressure squeezes.

Jimmy explained the rules: Each team had to select one captain to represent them. That captain would soon face a decision that would test not just their courage but their loyalty.

Before our team made any moves, I got down on one knee and prayed once again. "Father, whatever this challenge brings, give me discernment. Give our team unity. And let Your will be done."

When I opened my eyes, the choice for our team was already clear. All of us turned to Jeff. There wasn't even a question. We knew his heart. We knew his integrity. And we knew that no amount of money could tempt him.

Jeff had already won *Beast Games* Season 1 and taken home ten million dollars—but more importantly, he'd already proven that his faith and character were priceless.

The other teams weren't so sure of themselves. You could see the debate in their eyes—some whispering, some second-guessing. Trust suddenly became a rare commodity.

Finally, the captains were chosen: Team One chose JT. Team Two chose Hannah. Team Four chose Nick. Team Five chose Tyler.

Jimmy's grin widened. The tension was thick enough to cut through.

And then the magic—and madness—began.

The giant screen lit up with a glowing money counter that began to rise. Slowly at first—$10,000 . . . $50,000 . . . $100,000. Then faster—$250,000, $500,000. The sound of the counter echoed across the city like thunder, building suspense with every passing second.

Contestants shifted nervously. Hands went to faces. Some laughed uneasily. Others whispered prayers of their own.

I watched the numbers climb and thought about my own life. A million dollars could have cleared every bad flip, every loan, every overdue notice. It could've erased the visible evidence of my worst financial decisions.

But it couldn't erase the *lesson*.

Money can erase a bill, but it can't erase the moment you chose fear over wisdom.

It can ease pressure, but it can't replace the character you lost chasing relief.

It can change your circumstances, but it can't change your soul.

That was the difference between the prize and the purpose. And in that moment, I understood more clearly than ever: This whole game was a test of what five million can't buy.

And then it happened—the counter hit one million.

Without hesitation, JT slammed his hand down on the button.

The sound was sharp, echoing across the sand pit. He immediately dropped to one knee, maybe in regret, maybe trying to hide from the glares he knew were coming.

The silence that followed was deafening.

And then—the firestorm.

From his podium down below, his teammates Mia, John, Brandon, and Luke erupted. Shock, anger, disbelief—it all poured out in a wave. Their shouts echoed through the city, their faces full of heartbreak. You could feel the sting of betrayal in the air.

I stood there in awe—not judging, just quietly taking it all in. It was a moment that said more about human nature than any words ever could. Temptation has a way of testing us all. I understood the pull. I understood the pressure. I understood how, in a single moment, a big number can feel like the easiest way to fix years of pain.

But I also understood something else: If you take the money and compromise your character, you don't really fix anything. You just magnify the cracks.

As the dust settled, I closed my eyes and whispered, "Lord, keep me steady. Keep my heart pure. Help me always choose faith over fortune. Never let me trade what You're building in me for a shortcut that only looks like relief."

Because in *Beast Games*, just like in life, the real prize isn't the money.

It's keeping your integrity when the world tells you to sell it.

And that . . . is what five million can't buy.

"Let integrity and uprightness preserve me,
For I wait for You."

Psalm 25:21

Chapter 9
THE CANNONBALL CHALLENGE

Running toward the unknown

"Faith moves fastest when certainty is absent."

The next evening, as the sky shifted from orange to deep purple and Beast City prepared to settle into its night rhythm, Jimmy's voice blasted across the speakers calling every contestant to gather by the gym. Anytime his voice carried that tone—firm, energized, urgent—you knew something major was about to unfold.

We all made our way over, exchanging curious glances. The gym lights illuminated the area like a stadium before kickoff. We stood shoulder to shoulder, adrenaline already beginning to stir even before we knew what we were in for.

Then came the rumble.

Two massive cranes, towering like mechanical giants, began lifting the Conex walls straight upward. Metal groaned. Dust spiraled into the air. A few contestants shielded their eyes as the lights hit the steel mid-air. And the moment the wall cleared the set behind it, the crowd collectively froze.

Before us stood a scene straight out of a movie: ten giant cannons, lined up in perfect formation, each one aimed at a mountain of wooden crates branded with bold black and red TNT stamps. It looked chaotic, dangerous, and thrilling all at once—the kind of moment only MrBeast could dream up.

We whispered among ourselves, stunned. What challenge could possibly involve cannons and fake explosives?

Jimmy stepped forward, smiling like a man who had been waiting to reveal this twist all week.

"There are ten cannonballs hidden throughout the city," he said. "Your mission is simple: find one, load it, fire it . . . and earn the chance to compete for an island."

An island.

The words hit us like a jolt of electricity.

None of us knew then that the journey would take us thousands of miles across the globe to Fiji, stepping into challenges designed by the legendary *Survivor* production team. All we knew in that moment was that something extraordinary was on the line— another opportunity wrapped in risk, speed, and uncertainty.

And before the chaos began, I did what I have always done.

I lowered myself onto one knee, bowed my head, and prayed.

I prayed for wisdom.

For clarity.

For the Holy Spirit to guide my steps, just as He had been doing throughout the entire competition.

And I remember thinking to myself—even in a game like this, surrounded by noise, adrenaline, cameras, and competition—God could still speak. God could still lead. And I needed to stay close enough to hear Him.

Because money can motivate motion, but it can't replace discernment. And this game, I was learning, was revealing over and over again what five million can't buy.

I rose to my feet with a calm that only faith can give.

Jimmy raised the megaphone.

"Contestants . . . are you ready?"

A short pause.

"GO!"

The city exploded into action.

I ran full sprint toward the nearest building—turning tables over, digging through cabinets, scanning corners. I searched inside the Feastables Café. I tore through the library. I scoured every inch of the gym.

But nothing.

Then something nudged me—an internal pull I'd felt many times in my life. A whisper of direction. A gentle guidance from the Holy Spirit.

The sandpit.

I ran there without hesitation, dropped to my knees, and started digging like a man possessed. Something felt significant about that spot—something urging me to keep going. So I dug and dug, ripping through the sand with my bare hands, trusting that inner prompting.

Then the cannons began firing.

BOOM.

Another *BOOM.*

Then a third.

Each blast echoed across the city. Each one signaled someone else had found their cannonball while I remained empty-handed. Still, I kept digging. I didn't want to move. Something told me to stay.

But then my mind—impatient, logical, hurried—interrupted what my spirit had been telling me.

Maybe you're wrong.

Maybe it's somewhere else.

You're wasting time here.

And I made the mistake of standing up and searching again.

I left the very place God had stirred my spirit to stay.

Minutes passed. The field thinned. More cannons fired.

Then Jimmy's voice blasted across the loudspeakers:

"There are only two cannonballs left—and they are buried in the sandpit!"

My heart hit my stomach.

I sprinted back to the pit as fast as my legs could carry me. I dove back into the sand, digging with every ounce of strength. Sweat poured down my face. Sand caked under my nails.

I clawed at the ground intensely, knowing how close I might be.

Then—just one foot away from where I had been digging earlier—

"I FOUND ONE!" Kadie shouted, raising the cannonball overhead.

I froze. My heart dropped.

I had been right there.

God had led me there.

The Holy Spirit had guided me to that very spot.

And I had talked myself out of trusting the nudge.

If I had just dug a little longer . . .

If I had ignored the doubt . . .

If I had trusted God instantly instead of eventually . . .

That cannonball could have been mine.

Before I could even process the sting, another voice rang out from the opposite side of the pit.

"FOUND ONE!"

JC.

The last cannonball.

And just like that, it was over.

Ten cannonballs found. Ten people headed to Fiji. Ten chances gone.

The rest of us sat together in a quiet row of disappointment—contestants who felt the weight of coming so close only to fall short. I could see it in their eyes, and they could see it in mine.

For a moment, I felt defeated—truly defeated.

But then something inside me shifted.

A reminder. A truth. A lesson this moment was meant to carve deeper into my heart:

If God leads you somewhere, trust Him—fully, immediately, wholeheartedly.

So I dropped again to one knee.

This time, not to ask—but to thank.

"Lord, thank You. I trust Your plan more than the path I think I need. If You closed this door, it only means another one is opening."

And peace washed over me.

Not frustration. Not bitterness. Not regret—just understanding.

Because faith isn't proven in the victories.

Faith is proven in how you handle the moments that don't go your way.

And right then, I understood something essential—something no prize, no island, and no amount of money could teach me:

God didn't withhold that cannonball from me.

He protected me from something that wasn't meant for me.

And I realized that if I was going to make it through this competition—if I was going to stand firm all the way to the end—I had to trust God without hesitation. I had to lean on the Holy Spirit without second-guessing. I had to obey instantly, not eventually.

Even though I didn't fire a cannon that night, my spirit felt renewed.

And I walked away knowing this wasn't the end of my story. It was just another chapter in understanding what five million can't buy.

"But the Helper, the Holy Spirit,
whom the Father will send in My name,
He will teach you all things,
and bring to your remembrance
all things that I said to you."

John 14:26

Chapter 10
WAITING
WHILE OTHERS COMPETE

Learning patience in stillness

"Waiting is not wasted time—it is preparation."

The moment the other ten left Beast City to fly halfway across the world, Beast City felt . . . quieter. Not empty—just different. Ten of us remained behind, watching as the nice white limousine carried the other ten out of the lot toward a challenge none of us even knew existed yet. One moment, they were standing beside us; the next, they were heading for Fiji to compete for an island like something straight out of *Survivor*. We stayed behind, told to rest, recover, and wait. That might sound relaxing. It wasn't. Waiting in Beast City was its own kind of pressure—its own mental challenge.

Waiting has a way of bringing clarity. When the noise fades and the movement stops, it becomes easier to see that what truly matters was never meant to be measured by speed, spectacle, or prize money in the first place.

But Jimmy and T-Mobile must've already foreseen that heaviness, the fog creeping into our minds as we wondered what the others were doing, how intense their challenges were, and whether they'd return. So they made Beast City feel . . . alive again. Every day, something new appeared like a birthday where you didn't know what gifts were coming.

One day, it was a gourmet sushi chef rolling out trays of perfectly cut sashimi and stacked rolls, as if we were dining seaside in Japan instead of in a giant manufactured city. Another day, professional hairstylists strolled through the doors with scissors shining under the studio lights, trimming up fades and lining us out so we looked halfway presentable for whatever madness was coming next. Another morning, a couple of masseuses arrived, working on the knots in our backs and shoulders, the tension that had built from weeks of stress, running, climbing, competing, and praying our way through the chaos.

It was generous. It was surreal. And yet, even surrounded by comfort, I was reminded that peace doesn't come from being entertained or distracted. Peace comes from knowing who you are when nothing is demanded of you.

We got movie nights with popcorn and candy—real popcorn, the kind that smells like childhood and county fairs. A golf simulator appeared one afternoon, and suddenly we were driving balls into a virtual Pebble Beach like retired athletes with nothing but time.

But the best thing—the thing that lit all of us up—was the pickleball court.

It became our sanctuary. Sun-up to late-night under the neon glow, paddles cracking, feet sliding, laughter bouncing off the walls of Beast City like echoes in a tiny universe that only we inhabited. Pickleball was where we forgot about strategy, forgot about money, forgot about cameras. It was pure joy. Pure fellowship. For those few days, we weren't contestants; we were brothers and sisters trying to keep our sanity.

In a game built around millions of dollars, it was striking how quickly joy returned when money stopped being the focus. I was already learning the lessons of what five million can't buy, long before the final outcome was ever decided.

Then the vans rolled back in.

The ten contestants who had flown to Fiji stepped out looking like they had traveled through time—sun-kissed, exhausted, energized, shaken, and proud, all at the same time. They gathered us around and told us the news: Ian had won the island.

But the surprises weren't done. Jimmy then told all of us that JC had earned a coin for being runner-up for the island—a single coin he could flip at a later time to potentially double the jackpot to ten million dollars. You would've thought someone had handed him the keys to the universe. And maybe they did. *Beast Games* has a way of making one moment feel like destiny.

Then, just as quickly as the other ten contestants arrived back in Beast City, Jimmy summoned us to the basketball courts. We lined up shoulder to shoulder, and the walls dropped open like a stage reveal.

And there they were.

The red cubes.

The same suffocating red cubes from Season One. The same cubes where people walked in . . . and not everyone walked out. Just seeing them sent a pulse of dread down my spine. It didn't matter if you were strong or brave or faithful—those cubes had a spiritual weight to them. They tested something deeper than muscles. They tested your will.

Jimmy told us we'd form teams of three.

Without hesitation, Brett and I locked eyes with JT. There was never a question. We had become a trio—aligned in mindset, faith, work ethic, and heart. So we paired up. The brotherhood was sealed with a nod.

Then the twist came.

Before we entered the cubes, Jimmy explained that each cube had a phone—a magical phone with one rule: You can order anything you want, but it cannot leave the red cube.

Anything.

So we turned into kids with unlimited wishes.

"Pizza?"

"Got it."

"Energy drinks?"

"Absolutely."

"Football? Basketball? Playing cards?"

"Yep, send it."

Then JT joked, "Can we order a tiger?"

We'd heard rumors that Jimmy had rented a tiger for another video, so we shot our shot.

The answer came back: "We can't bring in the tiger."

We laughed so hard we cried.

Then came the moment that changed everything.

We'd been sitting in the red cube for several hours when JT pulled Brett and me aside. His face was steady, but his eyes were heavy with something holy—something deeper than strategy or competition.

He said he wanted to sacrifice himself so Brett and I could continue.

He had already won one million dollars in the Captain's Bribe. He didn't want to take the chance from us. He wanted to stand in the gap.

It hit us like a wave.

Three grown men—competitors, warriors, battle-tested— standing there with tears welling up, because in that moment, this wasn't a game. This was love. Brotherhood. Sacrifice. The kind of wealth no prize pool could ever replace.

I used to wonder, watching Season One, why contestants cried when they had only known each other for a short time. But now I understood. When you take away phones, TVs, computers—when the world goes quiet and distractions disappear—you see people's souls. You talk about life, pain, dreams, trauma. You bond like soldiers in combat, because in a way, this *was* combat. Emotional, spiritual, mental combat. A battle of endurance and identity.

And we had been living this together for a month. What looks quick on TV is agonizingly long in reality. Every day chips away at your walls, and every conversation builds something new between you.

As JT prepared for the sacrifice, Brett picked up a guitar we'd ordered and started playing Zach Bryan songs, the chords floating through the air like a soundtrack to our heartbreak. A barber—we had ordered one with our special phone—was trimming up JT's hair right there on the spot, and that simple act made the moment even more emotional. It felt intimate, symbolic—like he was being groomed for something solemn, something sacrificial.

JT sat still, eyes closed, tears slipping from the corners.

Tears started to fall from my own eyes too—not from fear or loss, but from the weight of love, sacrifice, and brotherhood filling that small white room.

Brett strummed.

I stood there praying—asking God for peace, strength, and clarity for all of us.

And then JT handcuffed himself to the wall so Brett and I could continue our race.

I'll never forget that moment.

I'll never forget the courage it took. The humility. The selflessness. The brotherhood.

It was one of the most honorable things I've ever witnessed in my life.

I hold an enormous amount of respect for JT for giving us that chance—choosing our path over his own. That's something you don't forget. Something you carry forever.

Because *Beast Games* isn't just a competition.

It's a crucible.

It's where people's true character rises to the surface.

Where faith meets fire.

Where strangers become brothers.

And where you learn—without question—what five million dollars can never buy.

"Greater love has no one than this,
than to lay down one's life for his friends."

John ¹5:13

Chapter 11
Thirteen Hearts

When everything becomes fragile

"What you protect reveals what you value."

The transition from twenty to thirteen felt different than all the other eliminations that came before it. It wasn't just another step forward; it felt like stepping into a narrower hallway, a funnel where every breath mattered, every prayer mattered, and every choice could shift the direction of a destiny. With only thirteen contestants left, the air in Beast City carried a strange mixture of excitement and heaviness. I could feel it in my chest, almost like a weight pressing down and lifting me up at the same time.

Every morning, as I opened my eyes in that strange, surreal world we were living in, I thanked God for the strength to keep going—because my body was tired, my muscles were beaten, my sciatica was ever-present, and mentally I was stretched thinner than I'd ever been. But my spirit? My spirit was on fire. God had kept me going this far, and I knew without a shadow of a doubt that He wasn't bringing me this close to the finish line just to leave me empty-handed.

Still, I was beginning to understand something deeper: even standing this close to five million dollars, there were things already taking shape inside me that money could never touch— faith under pressure, brotherhood forged in fire, and an unshakeable confidence rooted in obedience, not outcome.

I felt His presence in every challenge, in every quiet moment before the cameras rolled, in every breath between one heartbeat and the next. And I was grateful—more grateful than words could ever carry. Grateful for the opportunity. Grateful for the chance to fight. Grateful to be standing among thirteen extraordinary competitors, knowing that I was living a chapter of my life that people dream about.

But none of us could make it to the top alone.

That's why Brett and I found ourselves sitting down one night with Tyler, Nick, Auguste, and Jack. The six of us circled together with the neon lights of Beast City glowing across our faces. In that moment, we weren't contestants clawing toward a jackpot. We were brothers intent on pushing each other to the mountaintop. This alliance—this promise to help one another get to the top ten—was critical. We all felt it. We all knew the power of unity in a place built to divide.

Money could motivate people here. It could tempt them. It could fracture trust in an instant. But unity—real unity— couldn't be bought. It had to be chosen.

And that alliance, forged in whispers and illuminated by neon, would soon be tested harder than any of us expected.

***

Jimmy called all thirteen of us over to one of the Beast fields. It was the same field that sat directly in front of the massive five-million-dollar tower—the glowing centerpiece of Beast City. The tower shimmered in the sunlight like a monument to a dream only one of us would touch.

I stared at it for a moment longer than I meant to—not with hunger but with perspective. Five million dollars could change circumstances. But it couldn't create courage. It couldn't manufacture integrity. It couldn't replace faith.

"Contestants," Jimmy said, motioning toward the line of podiums that stood waiting for us like silent judges. "Stand behind a podium."

We each stepped into position, the tension building.

Then Jimmy's voice cut through the stillness:

"Guards . . . bring out the hearts."

Thirteen guards emerged in perfect formation, each carrying a large red glass heart—bright, beautiful, and heavy with meaning. They placed them gently on our podiums. We looked at each other, confused, unsure of what was coming next.

"These hearts represent your lives in *Beast Games*," Jimmy said. "When your heart is broken . . . you are eliminated."

A chill ran through all of us.

Then he added, "There will be two challenges. The winner of each challenge will team up together and decide which three hearts will be broken."

Silence. Absolute silence.

This wasn't about money anymore. This was about responsibility. About stewardship. About the weight of power in human hands—and whether character would hold when pressure squeezed tight.

We were blindfolded and escorted to our first challenge.

The ground beneath my feet changed from dirt to metal stairs, and the wind grew stronger the higher we seemed to walk.

When Jimmy finally told us to remove our blindfolds, the sight stole the breath straight from my lungs.

We were standing on a massive platform attached to a crane. Directly in front of us was a thick rope-wrapped pole suspended in the air. On my left was Monika. On my right was Nick. Next to Nick were Jack, Kadie, and Hannah. Across from us, forming the other half of a giant U-shape, the remaining contestants stood on another stage. Jimmy was on a third platform, completing the U.

Then Jimmy said, "Raise it up." The cranes groaned and lifted all three platforms one hundred feet into the sky. The entire city below shrank until people looked like toy figures.

My heart pounded, but not from fear—from purpose. From faith.

Once we were stabilized in the air, Jimmy looked at Monika and said, "I'll give you one hundred thousand dollars for the ten-million-dollar coin."

She didn't even hesitate. "No."

Money rained down as Jimmy shoved the stacks off the edge of his platform, letting them scatter into the wind like confetti. Then he told us the rules: three buzzers would sound. On the third buzzer, our platform would automatically release. We had to jump to the pole, cling on with everything we had, and hold until the buzzer sounded again.

Before the game started, I dropped to one knee—as I always did—and prayed for God's strength, protection, and victory. Then I stood up, kissed my hand, pointed to the sky, and said silently, *All glory is Yours, Lord.*

The buzzer went off. Then again. On the second sound, I leapt to the pole. Immediately, I realized this wasn't what I expected. The rope was so thick that it was hard to grip. The gloves made it worse, sliding against the fibers.

The pole felt like it was fighting me. But I clenched down. I blocked everything out. I repeated in my mind: *God is with me. God is with me. God is with me.*

Out of the corner of my eye, I saw Nick sliding. Instinctively— because helping others is in my DNA—I encouraged him. "You got this, brother! Hold on!" I kept encouraging him, pushing him, lifting him up with my words even from five feet away.

And then, in an instant I never saw coming, my foot slipped off the small round donut beneath me.

Suddenly there was nothing beneath me—only air. I dropped straight down like a skydiver plummeting from the clouds until the safety harness caught me and slowed the fall.

My stomach sank. My heart pounded. My whole left arm burned with rope burn—bleeding, raw, stinging.

I couldn't believe it. In trying to help my teammate, I lost focus. I fell first.

But even in that moment, as disappointment washed over me like a wave, I reminded myself, *God is still with me.*

I landed, took a steady breath, and dropped to one knee, thanking the Lord for His protection even in my fall.

One by one, others fell—Hannah, then Nick. But the battle came down to Monika and Brylee, locked in a duel of pure tenacity until finally Brylee slipped and Monika won.

"Great job," I told her when she came down.

"You're safe," she whispered back. Joy washed over me like warm sunlight.

When I slipped, when the harness caught me, when rope burn tore into my arm, I realized something painfully clear: strength alone isn't enough. Focus matters. Humility matters. And sometimes, even doing the right thing—encouraging someone else—can cost you.

***

The second challenge took place the next day. We walked into a studio where a massive stage stretched out before us—a giant floor made of LED panels glowing like a futuristic runway.

Jimmy explained the rules: we were to press our hands on the button to reveal the pattern. Once someone lifts their hand, the pattern disappears, and that person must walk it by memory.

One wrong step would equal elimination.

Then the pattern appeared. It wound across the floor like a wild serpent—wrapping left, right, forward, backward, curling around itself like a maze designed by a madman.

We tried to memorize it in sections, helping one another—a patchwork of teamwork under pressure.

Jim lifted his hand first, sacrificing himself. We guided him as far as our memory allowed before he stepped wrong and was out.

Then Catey went, and again we helped her forward until the pattern escaped all of us and she fell short.

Then Nick. He focused, trusted us, trusted himself—and we pieced the memory together like a puzzle. And then Monika, with perfect clarity, remembered the final stretch and guided him through.

As Nick crossed the finish line, relief washed over me. Gratitude followed close behind. Not because I was safe, but because I had witnessed something money could never buy: people laying themselves down for one another, trusting each other under impossible pressure.

***

Over the next forty-eight hours, Beast City softened into low conversations and strategic whispers. The Broken Hearts elimination was coming, and everyone pleaded their case. Everyone calculated. Everyone hoped.

But because my relationships were built on something deeper than advantage—built on honesty, faith, and respect—both Nick and Monika pulled me aside and said the same thing:

"You're safe."

I carried that promise in my chest like a warm ember. But I didn't cling to it. I didn't presume. I stayed grounded. Prayerful. Aware that nothing in this game—or in life—is guaranteed except the character you choose to walk in.

Finally, we stood behind our podiums again. Thirteen hearts glowing. The air silent, heavy, holy.

I dropped to one knee and prayed—not for protection, not for money, but for peace.

Then Jimmy gave the signal.

Nick lifted the hammer.

CRACK.

Brylee's heart shattered.

CRACK.

Tyler's heart shattered.

CRACK.

Catey's heart shattered.

Three hearts gone. Ten hearts left.

And mine? Still whole.

I whispered, "Thank You, Lord."

Because I knew something now that no prize could teach me:

Five million dollars could change my life.

But it couldn't buy the grace that carried me here.

"For by grace you have been saved through faith,
and that not of yourselves;
it is the gift of God"

Ephesians 2:8

Chapter 12
BEAST CITY AFTER DARK

Comfort in the middle of tension

"Even in pressure, God provides moments of rest."

The entrance tunnel to Beast City had never felt so heavy, so hollow, or so final as it did that night. Three hearts had just shattered—three bright red symbols of hope exploding into shards of glass on the field—and with their breaking, three more contestants walked out of Beast City for the last time. Their echoes faded behind the steel walls, and suddenly the vast city felt enormous again, almost too large for the ten of us who remained. Just ten hearts, ten stories, ten souls still standing in the greatest game ever played.

Ten.

I whispered the number under my breath, letting it settle into my chest like a prayer. *Father . . . thank You for bringing me this far.* Every day in this place required strength I didn't have on my own, and yet every morning, I woke up with breath in my lungs, fire in my spirit, and a peace I knew could only come from God. I felt His covering on me—guiding my steps, sharpening my focus, and holding me together during moments of fear, exhaustion, and loneliness.

Making the top ten wasn't just a milestone. It was mercy. It was grace. It was confirmation that I was exactly where I was meant to be. Standing that close to five million dollars, I was already learning a truth I couldn't ignore: some of the most important victories in life never show up on a scoreboard.

Season One had the families of the top ten flown in. Everyone knew that. Every contestant knew the stories—tearful reunions in the middle of Beast City, hugs that broke people in the best way. So naturally, more than a month into this experience, all of us wondered if it might happen again. But after the three hearts were smashed, and the dust settled, nothing hinted toward it. No winks from producers. No changes in our schedule. No whispered rumors among staff.

In fact, the opposite happened.

I was walking with Klitz after the eliminations, making small talk, when I said lightly, "Man . . . it would mean the world to see my wife and my three boys."

He didn't even blink. Just shook his head with a seriousness I wasn't expecting.

"We can't do families this year," he said. "Logistics. Way too complicated with the schedule and moving pieces."

And that was that. His tone wasn't teasing. It wasn't coy. It was final.

So I accepted it. As much as it stung, I understood. And honestly, I didn't press it again. I had already been away from my wife and boys for weeks—no calls, no texts, no emails, no little messages to say "I love you" or "I'm proud of you." Just total silence. A silence that stretched so long it started to feel like part of the game itself.

I missed them more than words could ever hold.

And in that quiet ache, I understood something no amount of prize money could fix: absence leaves a weight that only presence can lift. There are holes money can't fill, and silence that cash can't comfort.

***

When Klitz lined the ten of us up on the field near the entrance, none of us thought anything of it. We'd been in plenty of "B-roll positions" like this—stand here, look that way, hold still while they send up a drone. By now, this was normal.

The lights shone over the city, and the ground was warm beneath our feet.

"We just need some drone shots of the top ten," Klitz called out, adjusting his headset.

In unison, we turned toward the sky, facing the drone as it hovered above the five-million-dollar tower. The wind hummed past our ears. The tower glistened behind the camera like a monument carved from the impossible.

Just another day of filming. Or so we thought.

Behind us, footsteps pounded across the city floor—fast, sharp, urgent.

Before any of us could turn, two people rushed in from behind and grabbed Jim.

He screamed—not in fear, but in pure, electric joy. A sound so full of life it made all of us jump.

It took me a second to process what I was seeing. Then it hit me. His mom. His brother.

My heart stopped. No . . . no way. I was in shock and disbelief.

And then—I saw them. Three little silhouettes bursting through the entrance tunnel. Three little bodies sprinting with everything they had. Three little voices yelling, "Daddy! Daddy! Daddy!"

And behind them, my beautiful wife.

The world fell away. Beast City disappeared. The tower blurred. The drone might as well have fallen from the sky. All I saw were my four miracles running toward me.

I didn't hold back. I yelled, I laughed, I screamed their names, and then suddenly they were around me, on me, tackling me to the ground in a pile of love and joy and disbelief. I wrapped my arms around all of them, holding them so tight I could feel their little hearts beating through their shirts.

In that moment, I realized something with absolute clarity: this—this right here—was what five million dollars could never buy.

I had dreamed of this moment every night. But to have it happen right then—without a hint, without a warning—shook me to my core. Aside from marrying my wife and watching each of my sons be born, this was one of the happiest moments of my entire life.

I thanked God out loud, right there on the field, surrounded by my family and the bright moon and the cameras. I thanked Him for sustaining me through the silence, through the distance, through the ache of missing them. I thanked Him for this moment I didn't deserve but was blessed enough to receive.

No check, no trophy, no title could have matched the value of those arms around my neck.

I was overwhelmed by gratitude—not just to God, but to Jimmy, to Klitz, to Tyler, and to every producer and staff member who moved mountains behind the scenes to create this surprise. The logistics, the secrecy, the timing . . . it must have taken so much coordination and love.

And it meant more to me than they could ever know.

****

After the cheering and hugging and tears, I took my family on a full tour of Beast City. My boys ran around like they were in their own personal amusement park—eyes wide, mouths open, pointing at everything in complete disbelief that they were in the incredible place we'd watched together on TV.

They're huge MrBeast fans, so meeting Jimmy was like meeting a superhero. He talked to them, laughed with them, made them feel special. That meant the world to me. They also got to meet Chandler, Tareq, Nolan, and Karl—faces they'd seen on YouTube now standing right in front of them, shaking their hands, taking pictures, making them smile.

Seeing my boys beam with pride . . . man, it filled me with a joy I can't even describe.

Later that evening, T-Mobile and MrBeast hosted a special dinner for all of us and our families. The tables were beautifully set, the food was incredible, and they even played clips from our challenges on the massive screen while we ate. My boys kept pointing at me on the screen like I was the star of an action movie.

It was surreal.

It was magical.

It was a night I will never forget.

As I sat there with my wife's hand in mine, my boys laughing beside me, and the lights of Beast City glowing overhead, I felt this deep and humbling gratitude rise inside me.

God . . . You are so good.

This whole journey—every challenge, every prayer, and every moment of triumph—led to this day. A day of joy breaking through weeks of silence. A day of grace unfolding in the middle of a game built on intensity and pressure.

A day that reminded me, in the clearest way possible, that the greatest rewards in life aren't measured in dollars but in moments, in presence, in love.

A day where love walked straight into Beast City and found me.

And I will remember it forever.

"In everything give thanks;
for this is the will of God in Christ Jesus for you."

1 Thessalonians 5:18

Chapter 13
Buried Alive

Faith beneath the surface

"Sometimes survival means trusting God where you cannot breathe."

The night after the amazing reunion with our families, darkness settled over Beast City with a heaviness that felt almost prophetic, as if the darkness itself knew what was coming before we did. The air was cool, still, and strangely expectant when Jimmy's voice echoed through the loudspeakers, calling all ten of us to the sand pit. We exchanged quiet glances; no one knew what kind of challenge would happen after a reward like we'd just had. But one thing was certain: *Beast Games* wasn't done pushing us.

We gathered in the sand pit, a semicircle of shadows under the floodlights. Then Jimmy walked forward carrying a torch. The flame flickered against his face, setting everything around him aglow with an eerie orange hue.

"Light these," he said.

We each took a torch, touching our wicks to the flame until ten fires blazed in the night, crackling and spitting sparks. The smell of burning wood filled the air, mixing with the wind. Then Jimmy motioned toward the open gates of Beast City.

"Follow me."

Ten silhouettes, ten torches, walking down a dirt road in the middle of the night like something out of an ancient ritual. Off in the distance we could see faint lights glowing, but we couldn't make out shapes—just a soft, unnatural brightness gathered low to the ground.

We walked in silence, only the crunch of gravel under our feet and the hiss of our torches breaking the void. As the lights grew closer, the outline of something ominous began to appear.

A graveyard.

Rows of gravestones. Ten freshly dug plots. Ten coffins buried in the earth with electronic TV screens mounted above each headstone—screens that showed the inside of every single coffin.

Chills shot through me.

As we passed by each gravestone leading toward the ten caskets, we realized something haunting: every stone bore the name of an already eliminated contestant, along with an inscription describing exactly how they had been taken out of the game.

It felt like walking through the history of *Beast Games*, every name carved in stone, like memorials of battles lost. Standing there, staring at those markers, I realized how quickly a game built around money could turn into a reckoning about legacy—and how little cash matters when your name is etched into memory.

Jimmy stopped in front of the graves and motioned for us to line up. The torches cast long shadows across the dirt. The whole scene looked like a movie set from some ancient myth—ten warriors standing before their own symbolic graves.

"For this challenge," Jimmy said, "you need to pick one captain."

Nothing else. No rules. No hints. No explanation.

Just choose.

Nick and Monika stepped forward. Their faces were lit by flickering torchlight, determination etched into their features.

Jimmy said, "One by one, you will walk and stand behind the captain you want for this challenge."

Tyler, Auguste, and Jack walked behind Nick.

Kady, Hannah, and Jim stepped behind Monika.

Now it was Brett and me—the swing votes.

My loyalty pulled me to Nick—built on days of survival, alliance, and victory. I knew Monika could lead well. But I had given my word to Nick already. And in a place like this, your word becomes one of the few things that still anchors you—something far more valuable than any dollar amount.

So Brett and I stepped behind Nick.

Nick became the captain.

Jimmy nodded, almost solemnly, as if he knew what chain reaction had just been set in motion.

Then he explained the challenge.

"Nine of you will be buried," he said, "and the captain will decide the order you're dug up."

A quiet ripple of shock moved through the group. Buried. Underground.

The torches crackled. Someone exhaled sharply. The entire field shifted energy. In that moment, the challenge felt less like a game and more like surrender. We were placing our lives, our breath, and our trust into someone else's hands without knowing what awaited us on the other side.

I walked toward my coffin, with its camera mounted inside scanning back at me. Before climbing in, I did what I always did: I got down on one knee in the dirt and prayed.

Lord . . . give me strength. Give me wisdom. Give me peace.

And instantly, I felt calm settle over me like a blanket. Fear had no room in me when God's presence filled that space. I wasn't thinking about money, prizes, or outcomes—only about faith, trust, and obedience. I knew then that no amount of money waiting above ground could replace the peace I felt below it.

Then I climbed inside.

The lid closed. Darkness wrapped around me. Dirt started hitting the coffin—heavy, rhythmic, final. And then . . . silence.

Moments later, Jimmy's voice broke through the stillness over the microphone. He explained that there was one million dollars waiting at the basketball court—money that would be split in a familiar way, just like Season One. Contestants would take turns going to the pile and choosing how much to take. Some would take only their fair share. Others might take far more.

But about a week before any of us were buried, we had already talked about it. We had agreed—every one of us—that if this scenario came up, we would each take $100,000. Enough so that everyone could walk away with something. No greed. No shortcuts. Just fairness.

So when Jimmy made the announcement, buried beneath the earth, I couldn't help myself—I started yelling with joy. I was genuinely excited. I believed people would keep their word. I believed we were all about to walk away from that night with $100,000 in our hands and our integrity intact.

Before I ever saw a single dollar, before I ever stepped onto the court, I was happy—because I trusted Nick. I trusted the people who came before me. Each one had given me their word that they would only take $100,000, just enough so that everyone could walk away with something. That trust meant more to me than the money itself.

That trust was something money could never replace.

It felt surreal—the kind of moment suspended outside of time, where you're suddenly aware of every breath, every heartbeat, every shift of your body. Buried, trusting the people above ground, convinced that honor would win the night.

Thankfully, they gave us snacks and water. So we waited. We talked into the cameras. I shared stories about my military service—eight years, eight months, sixteen days in the United States Navy. My deployment to Iraq. The Riverine missions we ran day and night in our tactical boats, never knowing what we might encounter on the waterways. I talked about my wife. My boys. My parents and siblings. All the pieces of my life that kept me anchored even under six feet of earth.

Those were the things I held onto—not money, not prizes, not what might be waiting for me above ground. Love, faith, purpose. The things five million dollars can't buy.

Hours passed.

Eventually, exhaustion pulled at my eyelids. I started drifting off . . . wondering why it was taking so long.

Then finally—static crackled over the walkie.

"Cory," Nick's voice came through. "I'm about to dig you up."

Relief washed through me. Sunlight filtered through the cracks in the dirt as they began uncovering my coffin. When the lid lifted, the sunlight hit my face, and I breathed in the fresh air like it was the greatest gift in the world.

As Nick helped me out, he casually said, almost like it was nothing, "I took $250K."

Way more than his fair share.

At first, I brushed it off. I was just grateful to no longer be buried underground. But as Jimmy walked beside me on the way to the basketball court, asking if I'd still take $100K if it were available . . . something felt off.

"Yes," I said. "Integrity is the most important thing I want to teach my kids. I'd take my fair share."

But when I reached the court and saw only $235,667 left . . . fury shot through me like lightning.

If only Nick had taken more than his share, there should've been over $400K still there. But half the pile was gone.

Meaning someone—maybe multiple people—had taken more than they were supposed to.

The four people after me deserved a chance to take something home. So I divided the remaining $235,667 equally—five portions. I took my fair share of $47,133 left enough for the remaining four.

That felt right. That felt like honor. And honor, I was learning, is something money can never manufacture.

After everyone had gone through the process, Jimmy called us together for a full breakdown.

Nick admitted he took $250K.

Auguste took one-ninth of the total, equaling $83,333.

Tyler took $100K.

Jack took one-seventh of the total, equaling $81K.

Monika took $0 out of the pile of money.

Jim took $62,420.

Kady and Hannah split the difference and took $63,057 each.

And then Brett—my closest ally—confessed.

"I took $250K."

It hit me like a blow to the stomach.

My number one. My brother in this game. The person I trusted more than anyone.

Just the night before, he had met my family—my wife, my three boys. He knew exactly what I was fighting for.

I felt betrayed. Genuinely hurt. This wasn't strategy. This wasn't gameplay. This was taking money that should have gone toward my family, and the families of others, too.

I tried to hold it together, but emotion poured through me. I voiced my feelings to both Nick and Brett on the basketball court.

I voiced my feelings in the interviews. I didn't hide my anger or disappointment. I couldn't.

But even in that moment—when frustration, hurt, and disbelief swirled together inside me—I knew one truth: Anger leads nowhere good.

Wrath destroys from the inside out. Forgiveness is the only path forward. So I prayed.

And the Lord softened my heart. Not instantly, not easily—but enough to let go of the bitterness that tried to take root. Enough to remind me that every person in this game was fighting for something. Desperation does strange things to people.

This was *Beast Games*.

It was pressure, survival, instinct, fear, hope—all colliding at once.

In that coffin, when the darkness pressed in and escape was nowhere in sight, I learned that faith doesn't remove the weight. Rather, it gives you breath beneath it. Buried under earth and expectation, I began to understand something no prize could ever teach me: when everything else is stripped away, what remains is who you truly are.

And even though my spirit was shaken by the betrayal, I walked away with my integrity intact, my faith unbroken, and my heart aligned with the One who brought me here.

Often, the things that matter most in life aren't the ones you can carry out in your hands, but the ones you carry out in your soul.

And sometimes, that matters more than money.

"And let us not grow weary while doing good,
for in due season we shall reap
if we do not lose heart."

Galatians 6:9

Chapter 14

DESERT ROADS AND TESTED HEARTS

Speed, spectacle, and surrender

"God often tests us in places we never expected to go."

The desert doesn't just reveal what you're willing to risk. It exposes what you refuse to sell. It's a place where the shine of success fades fast, and what remains is what truly matters—the things no amount of money can purchase.

The flight felt endless.

Our double-decker airplane cut through the night sky like a floating city—two levels filled with cast, crew, cameras, and thoughts no one dared to say out loud. This wasn't a commercial flight with strangers and small talk. This was a traveling brotherhood. A moving sanctuary of competitors who had already endured more together than most people experience in a lifetime.

I tried to sleep. I really did. But my body wouldn't surrender.

Every time I closed my eyes, my mind replayed everything that had brought us here—the alliances, the sacrifices, the moments where faith carried me when strength ran out. The hum of the engines felt constant, steady, almost rhythmic, like a reminder that God was still moving even when we were suspended thousands of feet above the earth. No paycheck, no prize, no promise of money could quiet my spirit the way His presence did.

Somewhere over the ocean, I whispered a prayer into the darkness. *Thank You, Lord . . . for bringing me this far. Not for what I might win—but for who You've shaped me into becoming along the way.*

When we finally landed in Riyadh, Saudi Arabia, the doors opened to warm air and warmer smiles. From the moment we stepped off the plane, we were welcomed with genuine kindness—open arms, gracious hearts, and an unmistakable sense of hospitality. The people were friendly, respectful, and proud of their city. It didn't feel foreign. It felt intentional, like we were meant to be there.

And then we walked out of the terminal.

Ten Lamborghinis waited for us. Lined up perfectly. Each one a different color. Bright. Bold. Unreal.

For a moment, none of us spoke. We just stood there, exhausted, stunned, trying to process how real life could feel so unreal. My eyes locked onto a yellow convertible Lamborghini, glowing under the lights like something pulled straight from a dream. I didn't hesitate. I walked right toward it.

The Saudi gentleman driving the car greeted me with a smile that matched the city's warmth. Kind. Polite. Excited. As the engine roared to life, my heart did too.

Then we took off.

Ten Lambos racing through the streets of Riyadh, engines echoing between buildings, lights streaking past like a cinematic blur. As we passed other cars, I could see people scrambling—hands reaching for phones, windows rolling down, faces lit up with disbelief. They had no idea who we were. No clue why ten luxury supercars were tearing through their city in perfect formation.

Production was still secret. But the moment was anything but.

I leaned back in the seat, wind rushing past me, and thanked the Lord over and over again. For His faithfulness. For His provision. For allowing a kid with a prayer and a promise to experience something so far beyond what I ever imagined. And yet, even surrounded by speed, spectacle, and excess, I knew this joy didn't come from horsepower or headlines. It came from grace—something five million dollars could never replicate.

This felt like a dream. A double-decker airplane headed halfway across the world. Lamborghinis in a desert city waiting. God's fingerprints were all over it.

We arrived at the main plaza where the eSports World Cup 2025 would soon take place, and a short ceremony welcomed us in. This moment was very humbling. It reminded me how small I was . . . and how big God is. Fame fades fast. Faith doesn't.

From there, we were driven to the Ritz-Carlton, where we would stay for the next several days. Riyadh was beautiful, but most of our time was spent sequestered in our hotel rooms. Fairness mattered. Integrity mattered. The game demanded it. And I was learning again that integrity is one of the few things in life that costs everything—but is worth far more than any prize.

We did get one break—to go bowling.

There were ten of us left. Just ten. Laughing. Competing. Bonding. The camaraderie felt deeper now, heavier, because every face carried the weight of what was at stake. At this level, the game stopped being about money and started revealing character.

Then came the moment we'd all been waiting for.

We were driven far outside the city to a brand-new movie studio—state-of-the-art, massive, pristine. As soon as we walked inside, my mind started racing. You could feel it in the air. This place wasn't built for comfort. It was built for conflict.

Ten soundproof glass rooms formed almost a complete circle. Inside each room sat a red phone.

That's when it hit me. This was that challenge.

The one from Season One.

The phone bribe challenge.

My stomach tightened.

I knew immediately how I would play this—just like I play my life. With integrity. With honesty. With reverence for the Lord. I told Jimmy right at the beginning that I would not buy anyone's vote, and I would not accept a bribe for mine. Because winning at the cost of who you are is never really winning.

The rules were simple. Use the red phones to call other contestants. Convince them. Persuade them. Bribe them if you wanted. Only six out of ten would move on.

Before the challenge started, I did what I always do. I got down on one knee and prayed to my Lord Jesus for wisdom, guidance, and strength. I wasn't asking to win; I was asking to walk through it the right way.

The phones started ringing instantly.

Tyler called me and told me that Monika and Jim wanted to send him through first. I was surprised. Tyler still had $100,000 available for bribes if needed. Meanwhile, aside from Monika, I had the least amount of money left.

And that was by choice.

Earlier, when I'd had the opportunity to keep more for myself, I chose to divide the one million split evenly among those behind me—Monika, Jim, Hannah, and Kadey—so everyone could walk away with something. Monika took zero from the split, though she covertly accepted a five-hundred-thousand-dollar bribe on the basketball court for her coin that could double the prize to ten million dollars.

Technically, I had the least. Spiritually, I felt rich beyond measure.

I hoped people would see that. I hoped integrity would matter. I hoped they'd recognize that some things—trust, fairness, faith—are worth more than what fits inside a briefcase.

Since the votes were already leaning toward Tyler, I agreed to vote the same. Pressure crept in, but prayer stayed louder.

Then the game turned dark.

Hannah bribed Monika and Jim to secure the second spot. Jack bribed his way into the third.

In the next round, Monika gave me her word that she and Jim would vote for me.

But I didn't know that Auguste had gone behind me—offering Monika and Jim $10K each for their votes.

When I realized what had happened, betrayal hit hard. It stung. Deeply. But there was no time to sit in it.

I had a choice.

Play the game . . . or go home regretting it forever.

Then Jeff's voice echoed in my heart: "Play hard."

I knew instantly—God had placed those words in Jeff's mouth for this exact moment. Playing hard didn't mean losing integrity.

It meant fighting faithfully, refusing to surrender what five million dollars could never buy.

I went to Nick and offered more than Auguste. Nick told me he'd already given his word, and I respected that.

So I shifted strategy.

I started paying for future rounds. I paid Nick. Then Brett. Then Kadey.

Kadey broke down in tears from the emotional weight of it all. I hugged her and told her I understood. This challenge was brutal—not physically, but spiritually and emotionally. It stripped you down to who you really were when money entered the conversation.

Because of that strategy, I secured the fifth spot without going back to Monika and Jim.

The final round was chaos.

Brett paid massive bribes to Nick, Kadey, Jim, and Monika. He secured the sixth spot—but then learned Jim took his money and didn't vote for him.

The room was heavy. Exhausted. Silent.

And through it all, I thanked God.

For wisdom.

For endurance.

For carrying me through another impossible moment.

I was still standing.

Still moving forward.

Still in *Beast Games* Season Two.

And I knew—without a doubt—that every road, every flight, every hard decision was shaping something far greater than a prize. Something eternal. Something lasting.

Because this journey was never about what I could win. It was about discovering what five million dollars could never buy.

"Fight the good fight of faith,
lay hold on eternal life,
to which you were also called
and have confessed the good confession
in the presence of many witnesses."

1 Timothy 6:12

Chapter 15
THE MILLION-DOLLAR MOMENT

When temptation speaks loudest

"The greatest tests don't threaten your strength—they test your values."

Riyadh still hummed beneath us. Even inside the walls of the brand-new movie production studio, the desert had an ancient, steady, and unshakable presence. Beast City had offered a strange kind of peace, a rhythm we'd learned to live inside. But here, in Saudi Arabia, everything felt larger. Louder. Like the land itself was watching. In a place surrounded by spectacle and scale, I was reminded that what truly anchors a man isn't what surrounds him but what's rooted inside him.

Jimmy called us over.

At first, it looked unimpressive—just an ordinary wall inside the studio. Smooth. Gray. Forgettable. We stood shoulder to shoulder, facing it, unsure why this moment felt heavier than most. The air conditioning hummed softly, lights glowing above us like a false calm. I'd seen enough in this game to know that the quiet moments were often the most dangerous—the ones where character, not strength, would be tested.

Then Jimmy's voice cut through the stillness. "Open the wall."

The wall split apart, and the studio transformed into something biblical.

Light poured out. Music swelled. Before us stood a massive, multi-tiered stage stretching across the entire soundstage—four stories tall, each level climbing upward like a giant pyramid carved out of ambition and consequence. Stairs zigzagged up every tier. Spotlights blazed from every angle, reflecting off polished steel and coal-toned surfaces. It felt less like a game set and more like a modern coliseum planted in the heart of Riyadh—a place designed to ask one question over and over: *What are you willing to sacrifice to move forward?*

None of us spoke. We just stared.

Jimmy led us upward, level by level, past challenges waiting in silence. On one tier, three massive round cylinders sat hidden beneath black cloths. On another, unfamiliar mechanisms waited like unanswered questions. Every step higher felt symbolic—closer to glory, closer to loss. With each step, I felt the weight of the truth settle deeper: no amount of money could steady my heart the way faith already had.

At the very top, our challenge revealed itself.

A wide foam pit stretched out beneath us. Six large planks extended over the void—one for each of us. Across the pit, perfectly aligned with each plank, stood small pedestals waiting to hold our red glass hearts.

We already knew what those hearts meant.

Life. Survival. Everything.

Things no prize money could replace once they were gone.

Jimmy lined us up according to the order we were voted through in the phone bribe challenge. Tyler went first. Studying the planks, he trusted instinct. If this involved projectiles, the ends felt safer. He chose one.

Hannah followed and reached the same conclusion, stepping onto the opposite end.

Jack took the plank next to Tyler. Auguste chose the one beside Jack. Then it was my turn.

I paused.

Two options remained: the second plank from the end next to Hannah, or the center—wedged between Auguste and Brett, surrounded by inevitable crossfire. I didn't calculate angles. I didn't overthink strategy.

I listened.

With God guiding my steps, I chose the spot beside Hannah. I'd learned by now that obedience often looks irrational—but it carries a peace that no strategic advantage ever could.

That left the middle plank for Brett.

Jimmy explained the rules.

Each of us placed our red glass heart on the pedestal across the foam pit in front of us. The objective was simple and ruthless: we would break each other's hearts to eliminate one another. It was brutal clarity—because in this game, just like life, someone's progress often comes at someone else's expense.

Brett's eyes lit up. He was a former Division I quarterback at Princeton. He smiled and said, "Finally—a challenge I'm built for."

Jimmy let that confidence breathe for just a second. "Oh—and one more thing," he said. "You won't be throwing the balls. You'll be kicking them."

The soccer balls rolled out.

I didn't expect the surge of calm that washed over me, but it did. Soccer had been stitched into my life from ages five through sixteen. These days, I played with my three boys whenever I could. Muscle memory awakened instantly. Of the six of us, only Tyler seemed to share that familiarity. It struck me how God had quietly prepared me long before this moment—proof that preparation often happens years before purpose is revealed.

Before the first kick, I did what I always did. I dropped to one knee on that Riyadh soundstage and prayed.

I told the Lord He was my strength. My courage. My rock. I didn't ask for an easy path—only His presence. And I felt it. Deeply. A reminder that peace is something five million dollars can never purchase.

Tyler kicked first. His ball flew toward Hannah's heart. Then Jack. Then Auguste. Then Brett. Then me. Then Hannah.

I aimed for Jack—not out of anger, but out of loyalty. Brett, Tyler, and I had an alliance. And I had given Hannah my word that I wouldn't kick at her heart. Even without that promise, I wouldn't have done it. One misstrike, one bad angle, and my own heart could shatter. That would have been a devastating way to leave Saudi Arabia—not because of elimination, but because of regret.

Round after round, Tyler kicked at Hannah. Jack and Auguste followed. Each time the ball skimmed dangerously close to my heart, my breath caught.

Eventually, Hannah broke down. Tears fell as she felt targeted and overwhelmed. My heart ached for her. Even though I wasn't aiming at her, I felt the weight of the moment pressing down on all of us. This wasn't entertainment anymore—it was exposure. Pressure has a way of revealing what people cling to when the stakes are highest.

I shifted once, kicking toward Auguste's heart. Afterward, he leaned toward me and made an agreement: if I stopped aiming at him, he wouldn't retaliate. I agreed. For several rounds, I simply tapped my ball into the foam pit below.

But the danger kept creeping closer.

Balls began flying inches from my heart. My nerves tightened. Then Jeff's words echoed again in my mind: *Play hard.*

I realized then that faith wasn't passive. Playing safe wasn't the same as playing faithful. I had to play the game fully, or risk going home burdened with regret heavier than defeat. Because some losses follow you longer than elimination ever could.

So I didn't hesitate.

I set the ball down. Took one step. Kicked with everything I had.

The ball flew clean and true—and shattered Jack's heart.

Glass exploded. The studio fell silent.

The guilt hit instantly. Jack wasn't just a competitor—he was my brother. I crossed the stage and hugged him, apologizing again and again. He understood. We both did. Still, it hurt. Brotherhood doesn't disappear just because the rules demand separation.

But *Beast Games* doesn't pause for grief.

The rounds continued. Then Tyler did the same thing—no hesitation, pure instinct. His ball smashed Auguste's heart into fragments.

Watching Jack and Auguste leave was painful. We had grown close. But weeks earlier, we'd made an agreement: Nick, Tyler, Brett, Jack, Auguste, and me—we'd help each other reach the top ten. After that, it would be every man for himself. Only one could win the five million dollars.

Now, only four of us remained in Riyadh.

I whispered a thank-you to the Lord. He had carried me again. Not with luck. Not with money. But with wisdom, restraint, and grace.

There was no time to breathe.

Jimmy immediately called us into the next challenge—still inside the Saudi production studio. Four poles stood before us, similar to one I had slipped from earlier in the game.

Jimmy explained the choice. We could hang on the poles until someone fell . . . or take the mental route.

Sixteen colored blocks. A specific pattern. Memorize it. Rebuild it correctly. Get it wrong—and you're eliminated.

Brett, Tyler, and I exchanged a look. We knew instantly. This had to be teamwork. And teamwork, I'd learned, was one of the most valuable currencies in this game—one you couldn't buy.

I felt for Hannah—but alliances mattered now more than ever. And I knew she would eliminate Brett if given the chance.

We split the memory. Brett took the first six blocks. I took the next six. Tyler took the final four.

Before it began, I dropped to one knee again.

I asked Jesus for wisdom, clarity, and strength. I wasn't leaning on intelligence or experience alone—I was leaning on something eternal.

We jumped onto the poles. Jimmy stacked the blocks. I ignored the first six to avoid confusion. I locked in on mine, burning them into my mind.

Brett looked at me. "You good?"

I took one last look. "Yes."

He hit the button. The blocks fell. I closed my eyes and repeated the sequence over and over.

When it was time, Brett stacked his six flawlessly. I called out mine without hesitation. Tyler finished the final four.

Perfect.

Brett earned the decision.

With compassion and respect, he told Hannah she was eliminated. She accepted it with grace—a fierce competitor who played with integrity all the way to the end. I will always respect her for that. Integrity, I was learning again, was worth far more than advancing by force.

And then the weight of the moment hit me.

Only three remained.

Brett. Tyler. And me.

Standing there inside a Riyadh movie studio, surrounded by lights, cameras, and a desert nation that had welcomed us with open arms, I lifted my eyes upward.

Against all odds, my closest alliances—my brothers in this journey—stood beside me in the top three of *Beast Games* Season Two.

Only God could have brought me this far. No strategy, no shortcut, and no sum of money could have done what He did.

Hannah disappeared beyond the lights, and with her exit, the room seemed to tighten.

Before any of us could fully process what had just happened, Jimmy's voice cut through again. Calm. Direct. Unrelenting.

"Follow me."

The three of us—Brett, Tyler, and me—descended the pyramid stage to the level we had passed earlier. The one with the three round podiums. This time, there were no black cloths hiding them. No mystery left in the shadows.

They stood exposed. Three massive cylindrical stations, made of thick glass, each with an opening on one side.

Jimmy positioned us behind one podium each. Then he explained the rules.

Each of us was to place our hand into the opening and press down on the button inside. At first, the glass was crystal clear— we could see one another's hands, fingers pressed firmly, knuckles whitening with tension.

Then production flipped the switch.

The glass instantly frosted over, blurring everything. We could no longer see who was still in or who might have already let go.

Jimmy continued.

"The money counter will start counting up. Whoever is the first to remove their fingers from the button will take home the amount on the counter when they let go."

He paused.

"But here's the twist—you won't know if someone else has already released before you."

My heart pounded.

This was a challenge built on trust, uncertainty, and courage. And suddenly, the contrast was clear: money measured seconds, but character measured everything else.

And I was grateful—deeply grateful—that it was the three of us standing there.

Because of our alliance, there was no secrecy. No deception. No posturing. We talked openly, honestly, like brothers who had been through too much together to lie now.

Tyler spoke first. "I feel like I'm supposed to keep going," he said. "I'm here for the five million."

I nodded immediately. "Same. I'm staying in. I want to finish this."

Then Brett spoke. He took a breath. "I think this is my moment," he said. "I feel peace about walking away . . . but I want to see how high it goes first."

Jimmy looked at us. "Place your hands on the button."

We did.

The counter started.

$1,000. Then $10,000.

The numbers climbed faster than my pulse.

$100,000.

The studio felt silent, even with the hum of lights and cameras. My mind was steady. My hand was firm. I whispered a prayer under my breath—not for money, not for fear—just for God's will to be done.

Then the counter stopped.

$1,000,000.

Immediately, we spoke.

"I didn't let go," Tyler said.

"I didn't either," I replied.

There was a pause.

Then Brett's voice broke through, steady and resolved. "I'm going for it."

He lifted his fingers.

Just like that, Brett became a millionaire.

Joy rushed through me. Pure joy. I smiled so hard my face hurt. I knew Brett was engaged. I knew what this money meant—not just for him, but for the life he was about to build, for the family he was preparing to lead.

Brett ran forward and dove into the pile of cash.

A million dollars.

We followed him, laughing, throwing bills into the air, showering him with money like brothers celebrating a dream realized. It felt unreal. Surreal. A moment frozen in time.

And then it hit me.

As the bills settled and Brett stood there grinning, holding his future in his hands, a quiet realization settled into my soul.

I was one of the final two contestants.

I stood there inside a movie studio in Riyadh, Saudi Arabia—lights blazing, cameras rolling, heart pounding—and I bowed my head.

I thanked God.

For carrying me. For guiding me. For sustaining me. For giving me something far greater than what five million dollars could ever buy.

I didn't know what was coming next. But I knew this: I was exactly where He wanted me to be.

"Yea, though I walk through the valley of the shadow of death,
I will fear no evil;
For You are with me;
Your rod and Your staff, they comfort me."

Psalm 23:4

Chapter 16
WHEN THE LAST LIGHT FLICKERS

One decision away

"Sometimes the difference between victory and loss is one faithful step."

Out of more than 400,000 applications, only two of us remained.

That truth sat heavy and holy in my chest as the final day arrived. I felt overwhelmed with gratitude—awed, humbled, and deeply aware that I had been carried to this moment by something far greater than my own strength. Two hundred contestants had entered this game. Forty relentless days of pressure, pain, alliances, sacrifice, prayer, and perseverance had passed. Every sleepless night, every test of integrity, every quiet moment alone with God had led here. And as the weight of the grand prize hovered over everything, I also felt the underlying message this whole journey had been preaching into my bones: what five million can't buy is what God had already been building in me—character, conviction, endurance, and peace.

The finish line was no longer distant. It was right in front of us.

***

There was a long pause between the million-dollar bribe challenge and the final showdown. A strange stillness settled over the set, like the quiet that falls just before a storm breaks. Tyler and I were separated—placed in different holding areas to preserve the integrity of the game. No talking. No strategizing. Just silence and anticipation. In that silence, the money felt loud in my mind—but so did the truth: money can change a bank account, but it can't replace the presence of God in a man's darkest hours.

During that downtime, production brought me a simple meal: rice and chicken. Nothing fancy. Yet in that moment, it felt almost sacred. I ate slowly, deliberately, letting my heart steady itself. I prayed quietly, asking not for victory but for peace, clarity, and the strength to honor God no matter how this ended. Because if this entire story was going to carry the name *What Five Million Can't Buy*, then I wanted my heart to prove it—right here, when everything was on the line.

Eventually, the moment came.

I was blindfolded and gently escorted through winding hallways toward the stage. I could hear the hum of lights, the faint movement of cameras, the echo of footsteps on steel. My pulse thundered in my ears. Then Jimmy's voice rang out, commanding and unmistakable: "Remove your blindfolds."

When the fabric lifted, my breath caught.

There it was—the final challenge.

The same one from Season One. The same challenge where Jeff had guessed the correct briefcase on his very first try. A large circular table stood before us, capable of spinning smoothly in either direction. Ten silver briefcases formed a perfect ring around it, each identical, each capable of holding a five-million-dollar check—or nothing at all. And staring at those cases, I realized again: five million could change my circumstances, but it couldn't define my worth. It couldn't purchase peace. It couldn't buy integrity. It couldn't replace the way God had carried me through every test.

Jimmy explained the rules with deliberate clarity. One player would hide the $5 million check in one briefcase. The other would ask questions, searching for any tell—any flicker of hesitation, change in tone, or nervous movement—to determine where the check was hidden.

Before the challenge began, I did as I always do before a challenging moment: I got down on one knee and prayed for peace, clarity and strength. Because this moment wasn't just about choosing a briefcase—it was about choosing who I would be under the brightest lights and the heaviest pressure.

A coin was flipped.

I gave Tyler the choice: heads or tails.

"Heads," he said.

The coin landed on tails.

I went first.

I turned my back and placed the blindfold on again. I could hear Tyler moving the briefcases—metal scraping softly against the table—but I had no idea what his strategy was. After a moment, he said he was finished. Jimmy instructed me to turn around and remove the blindfold.

Three briefcases sat untouched on the carousel.

Immediately, I dismissed them. Too obvious.

In the center were three stacks: one stack of two, one stack of one, and one stack of four. The stack of four felt logical—almost too logical. I narrowed my focus to two briefcases within that stack: number 6 and number 8.

Then the interrogation began.

I asked question after question, watching Tyler closely—his eyes, his breathing, his posture. I touched each briefcase, studying his reaction. Searching for any crack in the armor.

Every time, his response was the same: "Open it and find out."

No change in tone. No hesitation. Nothing.

Normally, I would never have picked briefcase six, but something about it tugged at me. Throughout the game, six had appeared again and again. Jeff had won Season One by choosing number six. Patterns matter in games like this. History whispers. And I couldn't help but think that sometimes in life, we chase signs looking for certainty when God is really asking us to trust Him even without it.

I chose briefcase number 6.

I opened it with anticipation—

—and my heart sank.

Empty.

Jimmy asked Tyler which briefcase held the check. "Number 8."

My stomach dropped.

I had been one decision away. And in that moment, the sting was sharp, but it was also revealing. Because being one decision away from five million dollars made me realize how close I already was to things money can't buy: the love of my family, the respect of good men, and a faith that refused to crumble.

As each round progressed, wrong guesses were removed, increasing the odds—but also intensifying the pressure. Now it was my turn to hide the check. I decided on a different approach than Tyler's. I left all the briefcases exactly where they were—no stacks, no distractions.

Tyler turned around and began asking me questions.

I gave him the same answer he had given me. "Open it and find out."

I guarded my voice, my breathing, my posture. Any slip could cost everything. And I felt that old lesson rising again: money might be the prize, but character is the test.

He guessed wrong.

Then came another round. And another.

Eventually, I realized something about myself: I'm not good at bluffing. So I chose a strategy rooted in truth. If I didn't know where the check was, then no question could betray me.

I closed my eyes. I spun the table several times. With my eyes still shut, I fumbled until I found a briefcase, opened it, placed the check inside, closed it, and spun the table again.

I had no idea where the money was.

When Tyler turned around, I told him the truth—that I didn't know which briefcase held the check. Jimmy asked Tyler if he believed me.

He did.

And Tyler guessed wrong.

Round after round passed like this—two exhausted men locked in a chess match of faith, chance, and endurance. We had been filming all night. By now, it was 8:00 a.m. Sleep deprivation blurred the edges of reality. My body was running on fumes, but my spirit kept repeating the same anchor: no matter what happens, God is still good—and that's something five million can't buy.

Finally, only three briefcases remained.

It was my turn to hide the check. I spaced the three cases evenly around the table, closed my eyes, spun the carousel, placed the check blindly, and spun it again. When I finished, Jimmy told Tyler to remove his blindfold.

Tyler paused.

Then he said something that made my heart stop.

"I'm choosing briefcase number three . . . because you have three boys."

Time slowed.

He opened it.

Light spilled out.

The check was there.

"YES!!!!!!" Tyler screamed, sprinting toward the mountain of money.

I couldn't move.

I stared at the floor, frozen—shock and grief crashing over me all at once. In a single moment, every hope of erasing debt, every dream of helping homeless veterans, every prayer whispered in the dark felt like it shattered. The number was so huge it almost felt unreal—like losing it should've only been financial. But it wasn't. It was personal. It was generational. It was the weight of responsibility pressing down all at once.

It hurt in a way I had never known.

But even then—especially then—I knew how I had to respond.

With honor.

With humility.

With grace.

Because grace is one of the most valuable things in the world—and it can't be purchased, earned, or forced. It can only be given.

Jimmy came over. Tyler hugged me. I told him this was his moment—that he should be proud. If anyone deserved to win, it was Tyler: a devoted father of two, a man serving our country in the United States Air Force, a competitor of integrity and heart. And as much as it hurt, I meant it—because bitterness would cost me something far more valuable than money ever could.

Then Jimmy gave me the floor.

I walked up the stairs to the stage where this journey had begun twelve hours earlier. I spoke from the depths of my soul—grateful for the opportunity, grateful for the blessing, grateful for the experience of a lifetime. And even as my chest tightened and my voice fought to stay steady, I could feel the truth of this book's title settling into the moment like a signature: what five million can't buy is the ability to stand up straight after you've been crushed and still worship God.

Then I dropped to one knee.

One last prayer.

I thanked God for carrying me. For guiding me. For walking every step with me—even here.

I knew, deep down, that God had something greater in store. That faith isn't proven by winning, but by remaining steadfast when you don't. And I realized something else in that sacred ache: money can fund a dream, but it can't create a calling.

Jimmy shattered my heart—literally—signaling my elimination.

"Drop me," I said.

I fell into the foam pit.

As I climbed out, Klitz rushed to me, holding me as the tears came fast and uncontrollably. I was crying, hyperventilating, undone. He guided me gently away from the cameras, protecting my brokenness.

I've lost championships before. I've faced hardship. But nothing had ever hurt like this.

Forty-two days. Fighting not just for myself, but for my family, my team, homeless veterans, and anyone who needed hope that God still gives second chances.

And in that pain, I learned something eternal: My faith is stronger than I ever knew.

God was with me—still is.

And this loss . . . was never the end of my purpose.

Because if there's one thing I know for sure now, it's this: what five million can't buy is what God forged in me through the loss—an unshakable foundation, a redeemed perspective, and a testimony no check could ever replace.

"For I consider that the sufferings of this present time are not worthy to be compared with the glory which shall be revealed in us."

Romans 8:18

Chapter 17
THE QUIET AFTER THE STORM

Grief, grace, and rebuilding

"Healing begins when the noise stops."

The ride back to the hotel in Riyadh felt unreal—like my body was moving, but my soul was still standing on that stage.

The city blurred past the window as exhaustion finally caught up to me. No cheers. No cameras. No crowd. Just silence and the echo of everything that had just happened. When we arrived, I barely spoke. I nodded, thanked the crew, and walked into my room carrying a weight far heavier than my bags.

The moment the door closed behind me, I turned the lock and exhaled for what felt like the first time all day.

I went straight to the bathroom.

I filled the tub with steaming water and slowly lowered myself in, letting the heat wrap around my body. My muscles screamed in protest. The sciatica pain that had haunted me throughout the competition shot down my right leg—sharp, relentless, unforgiving. The kind of pain that doesn't ask permission before it demands your attention.

I leaned my head back against the porcelain and closed my eyes.

For a long time, I didn't move.

The water rose and fell gently against my chest as I tried to breathe through both the physical pain and the emotional aftermath. My body ached, but my heart hurt more. The final challenge replayed itself over and over in my mind—every decision, every question, every briefcase. One number away. One moment away.

I would be lying if I said it wasn't incredibly hard to lose like that—on the world stage, in front of millions, after giving everything I had.

There's a difference between losing quietly and losing publicly.

Public loss exposes you. It strips you down. It invites the opinions of people who know only a fraction of your story. And alone in that room, with nothing but the sound of water and my own breathing, I felt the full weight of it.

I wanted to be content. I wanted to be grateful. I wanted my faith to carry me the way it always had.

But I also had to be honest.

This hurt.

And that honesty mattered—because I knew something from experience that many people try to avoid: there is a process to overcoming adversity. You don't skip it. You don't rush it. And you certainly don't fake your way through it.

Adversity demands to be felt.

So there in that bathtub, I began walking through the process the only way I knew how.

First comes acknowledgment.

I didn't pretend I was okay when I wasn't. I acknowledged the disappointment, the frustration, and the grief of what almost was. I allowed myself to mourn—not just the money, but the vision I had built in my heart of what winning would mean for my family and for the people I wanted to help.

Then comes acceptance.

Acceptance doesn't mean approval. It doesn't mean you like the outcome. It means you stop fighting reality. I accepted that the result was final—that no amount of replaying or wishing would change it. And in that acceptance, something subtle shifted inside me. The tension eased. My breathing slowed.

Next comes reflection.

I asked myself the hard questions. What did this season teach me? What did it reveal about my character, my faith, my limits, and my purpose? I realized I hadn't been defined by one decision but refined by forty-two days of choosing integrity, humility, and perseverance when it mattered most.

Then comes surrender.

This is the part where faith steps fully into the room. I surrendered the outcome to God—not as a cliché, but as a conscious act of trust. I reminded myself that God's plans don't end at disappointment. Sometimes they *begin* there.

And finally comes resolve.

Resolve to get back up. Resolve to carry the lesson forward. Resolve to let the loss become fuel rather than a prison.

As the water cooled and the pain in my leg slowly dulled, a sense of clarity settled over me. I didn't feel triumphant. I didn't feel healed. But I felt grounded.

I realized something profound in that moment:

Winning would have changed my circumstances.

Losing had the power to change *me*.

And if my story was meant to inspire others—to reach people who had fallen short, been overlooked, or come painfully close—then maybe this ending wasn't a detour.

Maybe it was the assignment.

***

Eventually, the silence was broken again—this time in a private area of the airport in Riyadh, where all of us from *Beast*

Games—contestants, staff, and the production crew—were gathered to fly back to the United States. It was the first moment in weeks where the game finally loosened its grip. That's when we were given our cell phones back.

Holding that phone in my hand felt heavier than I remembered. Not because of its weight, but because of what it represented. Reality. Reconnection. Consequences. Everything I had held at bay while fighting my way to the final challenge came rushing back all at once.

I sat down and stared at the screen before turning it on. Notifications flooded in—missed calls, messages, reminders of a world that had kept moving while mine stood still. But there was only one call that mattered.

Home.

I pressed Carolina's name and lifted the phone to my ear, already feeling my chest tighten. When she answered, I heard it immediately—relief wrapped in restraint.

"Hey babe," she said softly.

Those two words undid me.

I told her everything. That I made it all the way to the final challenge. That I was one briefcase away. That I lost.

She was strong—stronger than I felt. She told me it was okay. That she was proud of me. That the boys were proud of me. But I could hear it in her voice, no matter how hard she tried to hide it. The pain. The disappointment. The weight of what almost was.

She tried to stay positive in front of our boys. She always does. But I knew better. I knew she was hurting the same way I was; she was just carrying it differently.

Carolina had made the ultimate sacrifice.

While I was gone, she ran everything. The household. The schedules. The emotions. Three boys who missed their dad. Bills that didn't pause. Problems that didn't wait. And she did it alone. None of our parents live close to us. There were no extra hands. No backup plan.

And there was no communication.

What hurt even more was knowing there was no runner-up prize. In Season One, second place had received $100,000. That money wouldn't have changed everything, but it would have helped. It would have given us breathing room. Some relief.

Instead, we were coming home with the same financial burdens—only heavier now because of how close we'd come to laying them down.

***

When I finally arrived at the airport back home and saw Carolina and my three boys waiting for me, everything else disappeared.

The boys ran as fast as they could, shouting at the top of their lungs—

"DADDYYYYY!"

They wrapped themselves around me, squeezing tight, and I dropped to my knees just to hold them. Carolina followed, pulling me into a hug that said everything words couldn't. She looked me in the eyes and told me she was proud of me.

For the first time since the final challenge, I felt like I could breathe.

***

Coming home didn't mean the struggle had ended.

The next few months were some of the hardest my family had ever faced. I've been on many deployments during my time in the Navy, so I understand reintegration. There's always an adjustment period.

But this was different.

To come that close to winning five million dollars—and to lose—cuts deep. And then to wake up each day, smile, and try to move forward with a positive mindset felt almost impossible at times.

The only way through was the process.

Acknowledgment.

Acceptance.

Reflection.

Surrender.

Resolve.

I leaned into it daily. The gym became my sanctuary—hours of movement, sweat, and silence where pain slowly turned into purpose.

But this experience didn't just test me. It tested our marriage.

Carolina and I were both hurting. Both grieving. Both trying to be strong for our children and for each other while carrying the weight of unresolved financial stress. There were hard conversations. Quiet tears. Long nights.

What saved us was putting God back at the center—not as an idea, but as the foundation.

We prayed together. We leaned on Him when we had no answers. We trusted that only God could carry us through something this heavy.

And He did.

This chapter didn't end the way the world defines victory. But it forged something deeper—faith that holds, love that endures, and resolve that no loss can steal the purpose God has placed on our lives.

The storm had passed.

The rebuilding had begun.

*"Let your light so shine before men,
that they may see your good works
and glorify your Father in heaven."*

Matthew 5:16

Chapter 18
THE TEN PRINCIPLES

Lessons forged under pressure

"Wisdom is the reward of experience properly examined."

After everything was over—after the lights dimmed, the crowd dispersed, and life slowly began to settle back into something recognizable—I felt an urgency to write.

At first, it wasn't for anyone else. It was for me.

I needed to make sense of what those forty-two days had carved into my heart. I needed to take the chaos, the pressure, the loss, the faith, and the growth and turn it into something I could carry forward. So I opened a notebook and began writing down the lessons Beast Games had taught me. Not lessons about winning money, but lessons about living well—about the things I discovered that five million dollars can't buy.

What surprised me wasn't how easily the words came; it was how clearly they spoke beyond the game.

These weren't strategies. They weren't shortcuts to success. They were principles.

And I realized something important: if they could hold up under the most intense pressure of my life—when five million dollars was dangling right in front of me—then they could hold up anywhere.

THE TEN PRINCIPLES

1. PLAY FAIR, ALWAYS – IF YOU COMPROMISE YOUR VALUES FOR A WIN, YOU'VE ALREADY LOST

There were moments in the game where cutting corners, bending truth, or justifying selfish choices would have been easy. Pressure has a way of whispering excuses. But I learned that integrity isn't situational; it's foundational.

A win achieved at the cost of your character will never satisfy you. Long after the prize fades, you're left with who you became to get there. I wanted to be able to look my wife and my children in the eyes and know I didn't trade my values for a moment of glory—because five million can't buy a clear conscience.

2. RESPECT YOUR OPPONENTS – THEY BRING OUT YOUR BEST

Competition isn't about destroying others; it's about being sharpened by them. Every strong competitor forced me to dig deeper, train harder, pray longer, and focus sharper.

Your opponents aren't obstacles; they're instruments of growth. Without them, you never discover how far you can really go. And growth, I learned, is something money can never manufacture.

3. DON'T CONFUSE THE PRIZE WITH THE PURPOSE – THE REAL REWARD IS GROWTH

The money was real. The pressure was real. The stakes were real.

But the purpose ran deeper.

Growth is the reward that can't be taken away. Money can be lost. Titles fade. Applause dies down. But who you become in the pursuit stays with you for life. Five million dollars can change your circumstances, but it can't replace the growth that happens in the grind.

4. LOSE WITH GRACE – IT SHOWS TRUE STRENGTH

Anyone can smile when they win. Grace shows up when you don't.

Losing with dignity, humility, and respect doesn't mean the pain disappears; it means you choose not to let the pain define you. Grace is strength under control, and it speaks louder than celebration ever could. And no amount of money can buy that kind of strength.

5. WIN WITH HUMILITY – REMEMBER HOW IT FEELS ON THE OTHER SIDE

I watched people win big—and I watched people lose everything.

Humility keeps you human. It reminds you that circumstances change, that today's victory could be tomorrow's lesson, and that compassion matters more than celebration. Five million can amplify who you are, but humility determines whether that amplification blesses or destroys.

Never forget how it feels to be on the other side of the scoreboard.

6. THE CROWD IS WATCHING – YOUR EXAMPLE CAN INSPIRE SOMEONE

Whether you realize it or not, someone is always learning from how you respond to pressure. Children. Strangers. People fighting silent battles of their own.

Your behavior under fire might be the courage someone else needs to keep going. And inspiration—real inspiration—is something money can never produce on its own.

7. YOU ARE MORE THAN THIS MOMENT – LIFE KEEPS MOVING FORWARD

No single moment, good or bad, gets to define your entire story.

This was one chapter, not the whole book. Life doesn't end at loss, and it doesn't peak at victory. There is always another step forward, another purpose waiting beyond the present moment. Five million can feel final—but purpose never is.

8. PRESSURE REVEALS CHARACTER – BE PROUD OF WHO YOU BECOME UNDER FIRE

Pressure doesn't create character; it exposes it.

When everything is stripped away, what remains is who you truly are. I learned to be proud not of my performance, but of my posture—how I carried myself when things didn't go my way. Character revealed under pressure is worth more than any check ever written.

9. DEFINE YOUR OWN VICTORY – DON'T LET OTHERS' SCOREBOARDS CONTROL YOU

If you let the world decide what winning looks like, you'll always feel behind.

Victory is personal. It's measured by faithfulness, growth, integrity, and resilience, not just outcomes. I learned to define success in a way that aligned with my values, not public opinion. Because five million dollars can't tell you who you are—you have to decide that for yourself.

10. NEVER STOP COMPETING WITH YOURSELF – THE TOUGHEST OPPONENT IS THE ONE IN THE MIRROR

The greatest competition isn't external. It's internal.

Every day is an opportunity to be stronger than yesterday, wiser than before, and more aligned with who God is shaping you to be. Outgrowing your former self is the most meaningful victory there is—and one that money can never outrun.

These aren't just rules for a game. They're a way of living.

Beast Games gave me an arena, but life gave me the real test. And if these principles can guide me through loss, pressure, and disappointment, then maybe they can help someone else do the same.

Because the true measure of a competition isn't who wins at the end. It's who you become along the way.

And that, I've learned, is what five million dollars can't buy.

The Whole Armor of God

10 Finally, my brethren, be strong in the Lord and in the power of His might.

11 Put on the whole armor of God, that you may be
able to stand against the wiles of the devil.

12 For we do not wrestle against flesh and blood, but against principalities, against powers, against the rulers of the darkness of this age, against spiritual hosts of wickedness in the heavenly places. 13 Therefore take up the whole armor of God, that you may be able to withstand in the evil day, and having done all, to stand.

14 Stand therefore, having girded your waist with truth, having put on the breastplate of righteousness, 15 and having shod your feet with the preparation of the gospel of peace; 16 above all, taking the shield of faith with which you will be able to quench all the fiery darts of the wicked one. 17 And take the helmet of salvation, and the sword of the Spirit, which is the word of God; 18 praying always with all prayer and supplication in the Spirit, being watchful to this end with all perseverance and supplication for all the saints."

Ephesians 6:10–18

Chapter 19
For Anyone Who's Ever Lost Big

Redefining victory

"Loss does not mean failure—it means formation."

If you've ever poured your heart into something—given it your time, your energy, your hope—and then walked away empty-handed, you already know how sharp that sting can be.

It's not just disappointment.

It's grief.

It's the quiet moment afterward when the noise fades and you're left alone with the question that hurts the most: *Was it all worth it?*

Maybe your loss came on a championship field, with the clock hitting zero and the scoreboard frozen against you.

Maybe it was a job you prayed for, trained for, believed was meant for you—only to get the call that said no.

Maybe it was a business, a relationship, a calling, or a dream you held onto for years that never materialized the way you imagined.

Loss doesn't discriminate. And it doesn't ask permission.

When I lost the final challenge—when five million dollars slipped through my fingers by one briefcase—I felt that same hollow ache. The kind that settles in your chest and makes the world feel strangely distant. The kind that forces you to confront not just what you lost, but what five million promised to fix—and what it never truly could.

Here's what I learned—something no victory ever taught me: Losing isn't the opposite of winning. It's part of it.

We're taught from a young age to see life in binaries—success or failure, win or lose, first or forgotten. But the truth is far more layered. Some of the most defining moments in our lives don't come with trophies or applause. They come quietly, wrapped in disappointment, revealing the difference between what looks like success and what actually lasts—between what money can provide and what five million can't buy.

Loss strips away illusion. It removes the safety net of external validation and forces you to stand face-to-face with yourself. It asks hard questions—about character, faith, resilience, and purpose—that winning rarely demands answers to.

Victory celebrates what you can do. Loss reveals who you are.

When everything was on the line, when the pressure was unbearable, when the world was watching—my loss showed me something priceless. It proved that I could stand in the fire without compromising my values. That I could walk away without bitterness. That I could lose publicly and still choose grace, humility, and faith.

That kind of proof changes you.

I didn't gain five million dollars, but I gained clarity. I gained perspective. I gained the unshakable knowledge that my worth isn't tied to a moment, a title, or a number on a check. I gained confidence that no matter how high the stakes, I can remain proud of the man I am when the outcome isn't what I hoped for—because you can't buy identity, peace, and self-respect.

And maybe that's what you need to hear right now.

If you lost big—if you came close and fell short, if you gave everything and didn't get the result—your story isn't over. You are not behind. You are not forgotten. And you are certainly not defeated.

Sometimes the loss isn't punishment. Sometimes it's preparation.

Preparation for deeper purpose. For greater impact. For a calling that requires more than talent—it requires character forged through disappointment. The kind of character that money can amplify but never create.

So if you're reading this with a heavy heart, know this:

You are not alone.

Your pain has meaning.

And this chapter, however painful, is shaping you for something ahead.

I lost the money. But I walked away with something far more valuable: The confidence that no matter what I face next, I can walk into it with integrity, faith, and my head held high.

And that is what five million can't buy—a victory no one can ever take away.

"I have fought the good fight,
I have finished the race,
I have kept the faith"
2 Timothy 4:7

Epilogue
THE GAME NEVER ENDS

"Every day is another round. Every choice is another move."

Beast Games Season Two ended the moment I walked off that stage.

The lights shut down. The cameras powered off. And five million dollars went to someone else.

But what followed taught me something I couldn't have learned any other way: money can reward performance, but it can't buy peace, purpose, or the strength to face what comes next.

In that moment, I realized the game wasn't over—it had simply changed form. There was no spinning table, no silver briefcase, and no towering structure built for spectacle. Now, there was only real life.

I woke up to responsibilities. To bills. To pain in my body. To healing that didn't happen overnight. To a marriage that needed patience. To children watching how their father handled disappointment. To decisions no one would applaud, but many would feel.

And I realized something simple and sobering:

This is the real arena.

Every day since I walked off that stage has presented its own challenges. They don't come with countdown clocks or dramatic music, but they test me just the same. They test my patience when exhaustion sets in. My courage when fear whispers that I came up short. My integrity when no one is watching and the easy choice tempts me.

That's the beauty of it.

The game goes on.

And so do I.

Life doesn't stop because you lost—or because you won. It keeps moving, offering new rounds, new decisions, and new opportunities to choose who you will be today. The question is never whether challenges will come. The question is how you'll respond when they do.

Will you play with integrity when cutting corners feels easier?

Will you show grace when the outcome doesn't go your way?

Will you stay humble when success finally comes?

Will you keep your faith when the scoreboard doesn't favor you?

The older I get, the more I understand that the most important competitions don't happen in front of crowds. They happen in kitchens, workplaces, quiet conversations, and private moments of resolve. They happen when no one is keeping score but God—and when the only prize is becoming a better version of yourself.

That's where the real victories are won. And that's where losses can still shape you for greatness.

If you've walked this journey with me—through the highs, the heartbreak, the near-misses, and the lessons—then know this: your story isn't paused. It isn't finished. It's unfolding, one choice at a time.

You're still in the game.

So am I.

And the next round is already waiting.

The only question left is the one that matters most:

How will you play it?

ACKNOWLEDGMENTS

There are moments in life when gratitude feels too small for what your heart carries. This is one of those moments.

First and foremost, all glory to God. Every open door, every closed one, every test, every triumph—He was there. What five million dollars couldn't buy was already given to me long before I stepped onto that stage: faith, peace, and purpose.

To my beautiful wife, Carolina—you are the quiet strength behind every bold step I take. You held our family steady while I chased a calling that didn't come with guarantees. You wiped tears at the airport, prayed over me when fear tried to creep in, and reminded our boys that Daddy was walking in faith. I love you more than words on these pages can express.

To my three sons—you are my why. Every challenge, every sleepless night, every prayer whispered under bright lights was for you. I hope when you read this one day, you don't see a man chasing money—you see a father chasing courage, conviction, and obedience.

To my family and close friends—thank you for believing in me when the path looked uncertain. Your encouragement carried me farther than you know.

To the contestants who became brothers and sisters—adversity has a way of revealing character. What we built in the pressure of competition was real. Brotherhood forged in fire lasts longer than any prize. I am grateful for every conversation, every laugh, every prayer we shared when the cameras weren't rolling.

To the crew, production staff, and everyone behind the scenes who worked tirelessly to create something unforgettable—thank you for your excellence and dedication.

To the readers—thank you for picking up this book. My hope is that you walk away reminded that success is not measured by a check, but by character. Not by applause, but by obedience. Not by what you win, but by who you become.

Five million dollars can change circumstances.

But it cannot buy faith.

It cannot buy family.

It cannot buy peace.

Those are gifts.

And I am eternally grateful.

About the Author

Cory Sims is a man of faith, a devoted husband, and a proud father of three boys who inspire him daily to live with courage and conviction. Known to many through his appearance on Beast Games Season 2, Cory's journey was never just about competition or prize money—it was about purpose.

Before stepping onto the global stage, Cory walked through seasons of financial hardship, hard lessons, and rebuilding. Those chapters shaped his resilience and deepened his dependence on God. His story is not one of perfection, but of perseverance—learning that true wealth is found in faith, family, and integrity.

Throughout What Five Million Can't Buy, Cory shares a behind-the-scenes look at pressure, brotherhood, prayer, and the quiet moments that never made it to camera. His words reflect a belief that life itself is the greatest arena, and that every challenge is an opportunity to grow stronger in character.

When he's not writing or building new ventures, Cory is investing in his family, encouraging others to walk boldly in their calling, and using his platform to remind people that success is not measured by what you win—but by who you become.

Some of the strongest warriors you will ever meet are still fighting— not on foreign soil, but right here at home.

Men and women who once stood ready to defend our freedom are now facing homelessness, isolation, and uncertainty. Warrior Wings Foundation exists to ensure they are not forgotten.

We help homeless and at-risk veterans rise from the streets into stable, dignified lives through housing pathways, essential resources, and personal support.

SCAN THE QR CODE
TO LEARN MORE OR MAKE A DONATION.

Your support helps restore hope, honor, and home to those who served.

Because no warrior should ever be left behind.

It is my honor to donate a portion of the proceeds from this book to Warrior Wings Foundation, supporting veterans on their journey from the streets to stability.

"Carry each other's burdens, and in this way you will fulfill the law of Christ."
Galatians 6:2